Shaping YOUR Family Story

Shaping YOUR Family Story

How Imperfect Parents Create Hope and Promise for Their Children

David W. Welday III
James L. Coffield, PhD

HIGHERLIFE
PUBLISHING & MARKETING

Shaping Your Family Story: How Imperfect Parents Create Hope and Promise for Their Children
by David W. Welday III and James L. Coffield

Published by HigherLife Publishing and Marketing, Inc.
PO Box 623307
Oviedo, Florida 32762
(407) 563-4806
www.ahigherlife.com
Distributed by Next Generation Institute, Inc.
www.nextgeninstitute.com

First Edition
16 17 18 19 20 — 8 7 6 5 4 3 2 1
Printed in the United States of America

Dedication

DAVID—I find it ironic—perhaps even comical—that I would write a parenting book. I am not a perfect parent, nor was I perfectly parented. But I will be forever grateful to my mom and dad, David and Sally Welday, for the way they loved me and raised me. In addition, I cannot imagine a more beautiful, wise and supportive wife and mother to our children than my bride, Amy. My three sons, David, Darren, and Jason each bring me such joy, hope, and blessing. I am so proud of you for the men you have become! Thank you for helping me become the man I am called to be.

JAMES—If all good stories are peppered with irony, I too find it ironic that I am co-authoring a parenting book. At times I have made the goal of being the perfect parent an idol, something too important. I have placed too much pressure on myself and on my kids. Being a father has been one of the greatest privileges in my life. I thank my wife Mona who has been so supportive and deserves credit not only for writing my PhD dissertation but helping me write this document as well. Though we sometimes changed the names in this book, I am profoundly grateful to Skylar, Pearce and Kim who are individually amazing people. You have each taught me more than I will ever teach you. If you ever wonder, know that you have my blessing.

Contents

Section Four: Protecting—
Creating a Positive Setting

Section Five: Correcting—
Conflict in Your Family's Story

Section Six: Connecting—
The Theme of Your Family Story

Note from the Authors

WHILE BOTH OF us have contributed to the content you are about to read, we recognize that it can be confusing for you to keep track of which one of us is speaking. While we have much in common, certainly our passion for parenting, we are very different people. One of us drives a sports car, the other a truck. One of us comes from a staunch reformed religious background, the other from the "wild and crazy" side of the spiritual tracks. We have different interests, abilities, and experiences. And yet we came together for this parenting project. So in the interest of making it easy for you to embrace the principles and information we hope to share with you, we have intentionally written in one voice. We want you to be able to relax and read without having to think, *Okay, is this David or Jim talking to me?* So, don't try to figure it out. May you find great peace and comfort in knowing that *you* are writing an incredible family story, one that can change the world.

Also, please understand that we have both spent years reading, hearing and learning from others, teaching about child development and attempting to practice what we learned. It is not our intent to claim that the thoughts shared in this book are original with us. Nor are we trying to avoid giving credit where credit is due. If confession is good for the soul, we readily confess that none of the ideas shared in this book are our own. We are humbly standing on the shoulders of others who have gone before us.

—DAVID AND JIM

P.S.—We've started each chapter with a common statement that most every parent says at one time or another. We did this by design to remind you that you are not alone. You're not the only imperfect parent who sometimes feels overwhelmed, unprepared, and not up to the task.

Preface

NOBODY'S PERFECT

David Welday had a goal and purpose. It had long been a passion of his to create a starting point for groups of parents to meet for the specific purpose of discussing parenting. Jim Coffield was rapidly approaching three decades of counseling with teens and adults when David first approached him about writing a book. David had been diligently working on this project for some time, but knew that Jim would be able to offer additional insights. We had no idea that two years and numerous rewrites later, this project would have evolved into this final form. Our collaboration has been filled with research, compromise, and persistence, not unlike parenting. We've had to choose our battles, agree upon the story premise, decide which themes are most important, and make difficult choices.

As in real life, and specifically the role of parenting, we have both remained true to the principles shared in this book while being flexible enough to allow our different personalities to be expressed. It is our goal to invite you to view your parenting experience through the grid of a story. We will discuss how to choose your themes, develop your characters, deal with the conflicts and direct the compelling story of your family.

Being a great parent is a high and noble calling. It changes lives. How you parent matters not only to your children and your family, but to your community—to the culture in which you live, and to generations yet to come. While we can all humbly acknowledge that there are no perfect parents, authors, or books, we invite you to come with us on this journey as we each attempt to write a better story for ourselves and those we love.

Remember, parenting is a process. Nobody gets it right all the time. We all make mistakes in our parenting. Just when you think you've got one child figured out, along comes another one with a totally different personality and set of strengths and weaknesses. But ironically, what can seem like failings and inconsistencies with parents or kids are not always a bad thing. In fact, sometimes our mistakes and failures can become some of the most important aspects of our child's development.

Great learning and discovery come through adversity. My former pastor Carl Buffington once said, "If it were up to us, we'd kill our kids." He went on to explain that as parents we have this idea that our love is best expressed by taking away all the roadblocks, obstacles, and challenges that our children face. If left to us, we'd spare them every heartache and trial that we've faced. Unfortunately, in doing so we'd very likely mess them up for life.

After all, who among us wouldn't want to spare our kids from pain and difficulty? Look at the amount of time we spend just trying to keep them out of trouble. But the truth is, wrestling with difficulty builds character. It makes us stronger. It makes us better. Much like a refinery's intense heat converts raw materials into something of value, life's difficult experiences refine us. So don't wallow in your mistakes—**let your refining moments become your defining moments.**

That's not to say you shouldn't endeavor to protect your children or that you should be complacent about being the best parent you can be. What I am saying is, don't beat yourself up over your shortcomings and failures. They just might be the stuff that helps turn your son or daughter into the next president, CEO, inventor, or great theologian.

While I hope this book helps you become a better parent, I think it's important to start our journey together by agreeing that there simply are no perfect parents, and you're not going to be the first. We all make mistakes, and those blunders can even be helpful. So relax. This is not a competition to see who turns out better kids—there is no contest (there shouldn't be, anyway) to see who wins the Best Dad of the Year award or the Mom of the Millennium trophy. We all win when we become better parents.

> *Let your refining moments become your defining moments.*

Hats off to you for picking up this book and getting this far. We hope you find the investment of time we spend together worthwhile. When you've worked through *Shaping Your Family Story*, feel free to contact us to let us know what you think about it.

—DAVID WELDAY AND JIM COFFIELD

Introduction

WHAT MAKES A GREAT FAMILY STORY?

A S SHE SAT in my office crying, she said she felt like her life was a character in a sitcom. Why would someone say that? Perhaps it's because we relate to stories. Stories captivate us. We identify with them and relate to them. Maybe you long to be William Wallace fighting for freedom or feel like the Tin Man in the Wizard of Oz who only wants a heart, or desire the tenacity of Katniss Everdeen who survives the Hunger Games. People often try to make sense of their lives by connecting to a character in story. We think in stories. We remember stories.

As a parent, what does it mean to write your family story? What story is your family telling to the world? In your story are you the hero, the villain, or just an unforgettable side character? Surely there are times when you will feel like all three. But you are cast in a key role. In many ways you are the director, producer, and writer all rolled into one. And while your story isn't

1

complete and the outcome is uncertain, you can make a difference—a huge difference on how it is written, and you can help your children become characters in your story who live life with purpose, passion, significance, and joy. That is a noble—even heroic—task, one that invites you to move from ordinary to extraordinary.

For generations ordinary men and women have inherited this profound responsibility. Some planned for it and some didn't. But it doesn't really matter how you got into this story. What matters is that you're here. And once you are in, you do your best to make your family story a great one.

Throughout this book, we will share some of our struggles with parenting. We hope that you can laugh at our clumsiness, share our successes, and grieve with our sorrows and losses as you embrace and catch the perspectives offered in the pages to come.

There will be days when you won't feel quite so noble about this holy calling called parenting. There are probably days when you will feel more exasperation than exhilaration over the prospect of being a parent. We all feel that way, but parenting is not about your feelings.

When it comes to parenting, people have all sorts of ideas about what "successful kids" look like: Is it how they behave? The kind of career path they follow? If they like us or not? If they make a lot of money? If they are happy? If they stay connected to us or become alienated?

It doesn't take much living to realize that simply being popular or having a lot of money isn't what life is all about. Being successful in life has a lot more to do with how you live than what you have or who you know. Being a successful parent has much more to do with helping our kids discover meaning, purpose, and joy in life—with helping them live significantly, confidently, and with a desire to make a difference in the world.

So how do you raise kids to live out such a grand story? Though there is no formula to follow or magic pill to swallow, there are core principles and practices that parents can follow to give them a better shot at raising successful kids.

To illustrate those practices, this book is divided into five main parts with each giving you a central principle to consider and hopefully put into practice. These five segments are:

- Reflecting
- Directing
- Protecting
- Correcting
- Connecting

Interestingly, these five segments correlate with the five crucial elements of a great story; **character, plot, setting, conflict, and theme.** As you read through each section, we hope you begin to see your role as a parent in a nobler light and we hope you will be both inspired and motivated to approach your role as a parent with a renewed sense of purpose and joy.

Section One

Ready, Set, Action...

Chapter 1

The Foundation of Your Family Story

"THIS IS NOT WHAT I SIGNED UP FOR— NOT THE DREAM I HAD FOR MY CHILD."

E VERYONE LOVES A redemptive story, one in which the unlikely hero wins the battle, the Hobbit carries the ring, the couple reunites after the war. We have also watched movies that do not seem to have focus or lack a clear plot. At the closing credits, we look at one another and wonder why we paid money to watch it. In much the same way, good or bad, the way we live life tells our story and the story of our family.

A family story may begin with dating and attraction and progress through courtship, newborn sleep deprivation, conversations in the principal's office, all the way to grandchildren, even great-grandchildren with all the hopes and tragedies that are sprinkled throughout. We will all eventually see our stories clearly as we look back. We will be able to see the different chapters, seasons, and themes, but once the story is written, it is very difficult to edit and change. **The time to make the edits to your family story is now.**

I wish I had considered this concept of my family being and living a story years ago. But even if your children are grown, it's never too late to start making your family story better. It is just easier to edit our stories early on when our children's minds and hearts are most malleable.

The Orlando Civic Center was packed. Thirty-six thousand people from around the country had descended upon Orlando dressed as Wookies, Star War Commanders, Han Solo, etc. From my perspective as a psychologist, it looked like a sea of mental illness. As my son and I walked around in awe of the spectacle that was the Star Wars Convention, we overhead a passionate argument. It was about whether an X-Wing Fighter would be able to withstand the pressure of achieving hyperspace. The arguing men (each in full costume) had become so angry that it seemed as if they were on the precipice of an intergalactic battle. Sadly, this passionate argument was about two things that do not exist, X-Wing Fighters and hyperspace. There is absolutely nothing wrong with Star Wars; it is a good story that has been well told. But it amazes me that so many people remain compelled by this story and its characters. As I looked over the sea of Princess Leias and Jabba the Huts, I was struck by the truth that people will be faithful to a compelling story.

The time to make the edits to your family story is now.

Good stories are evocative. They cause us to cry, to laugh, to hurt, to feel deeply about matters. As we consider our family and parenting, we want to purposely think about how we live out and direct a compelling story; a purposeful story that evokes life. As is true in each of our lives, good stories involve a character who wants

> A plane spends most of its flight time off course.

something and goes through great conflict to obtain it. People are faithful to a compelling story. May your family story be as compelling to your children as the Star Wars saga has been to so many millions.

As a parent, you are the principle director in the development of your family story. It's important to remember that what makes your story compelling and memorable is its imperfections and how you respond to them. For example, a plane spends most of its flight time off course. However, the GPS navigation system makes constant subtle corrections and so your flight arrives at its destination on time (well, some of the time). The analogy is applicable to our parenting. We mess up—a lot. Yet, if we make the needed course corrections all along the way, our kids have a much greater chance at becoming healthy, successful adults, despite our failures and short-comings.

You and I have our own individual stories. We are also part of a larger story made up of complex, interconnected parts. Like a solar system comprised of individual planets, families too, are made up of individuals living out unique personalities, temperaments, and values. These individual stories stand alone, yet are part of a larger story called family.

ELEMENTS OF A GOOD FAMILY STORY

A simple understanding of the arc of a story is given to us by Donald Miller when he tells us that a story consists simply of a character who wants something and must go through a conflict to fully realize it.

This book identifies five core principles that each relate to a crucial component of a great story. Here is a brief overview:

#1—Character (Reflecting)

The characters in a story are either static or dynamic. Static characters remain the same throughout the story while dynamic characters change. As a parent, you play a crucial role in helping your children grow and change in positive ways. A reflecting parent is more likely to produce characters that are dynamic— characters that mature, progress, grow, and change.

#2—Plot (Directing)

The plot of your family story is the order and timing of how the events of your storyline unfold. Most parents assume they have little say in these events and often find themselves merely reacting to circumstances as they occur. Directing or shaping your family story speaks more to the intentionality you use in helping your child find his or her way in life and proactively guiding them in the way they were designed to go. A movie that has good characters without a strong plot leaves the viewer unsatisfied. Much like a bad movie, a family that has no direction or purpose will often become shaped by whatever stories are being told around them, yet have no distinctive flavor of their own.

#3—Setting (Protecting)

The setting is the backdrop where the story takes place and includes the social, environmental, and religious components of the character's life. Compelling family stories create a safe, supportive, and sometimes challenging landscape in which to develop. In this text, we will call this protecting, because the world in which you are raising your children is not safe. It's glorious and wonderful, but certainly not safe. Our job as parents is to provide appropriate protection as we raise our kids in this world, which can be toxic.

#4—Conflict (Correcting)

Conflict is inevitable. How characters deal with conflict determines the outcome of the role that they play in their own story. How families deal with conflict and discipline determines much of the outcome of their family story. No parenting book would be complete without taking space to address matters of discipline and how to correct the wrong things we see happening in our family story.

#5—Theme (Connecting)

The theme of a story is the overriding message. A story's theme can also be described as the mission or vision that it carries. Every author writes with a purpose in mind—a message or feeling that they want to convey to the reader so that they walk away from the story with something of worth. Your family has a theme too, and it all has to do with how your family connects—with each other, with others, with their own history, and with God. What is the mission of your family? How does this mission play out in your daily decisions to connect?

NO CHILD (OR PARENT) IS AN ACCIDENT

The best stories usually have an element of surprise. While some children are carefully planned, many come along at inconvenient times and in less than ideal circumstances. Many of us simply don't feel prepared to be parents. You might feel you weren't parented well yourself, and didn't have a positive role model or memorable personal experiences from which to look back on. The story of your family is not random. I used to tell bedtime stories to my children. Along the way, they would add to the story often taking it in new directions from what I planned. But because they were part of the story, it held their attention. You may feel at times like your family story is unplanned, out of control or that you are just not cut out for shaping your family story. Please know that you were hand-picked by God, chosen for your role in your family's story. In fact, this is a role you were meant to play. This wonderful and complex adventure is not a chaotic or random journey, but a purposeful commitment that will include the greatest joys and sorrows of your life.

> *Much like a bad movie, a family that has no direction or purpose will often become shaped by whatever stories are being told around them, yet have no distinctive flavor of their own.*

If you believe that your existence is not an accident and that you are not a parent by accident, you will parent with more intention, faith, hope, and confidence. It matters how you raise your children and how you were raised. And though there may be some accidents along the way, there is purpose in our design.

Every parent questions whether or not they are qualified, capable, and equipped for parenting. You will be a better parent if you face this demon of uncertainty head on, wrestle him to the ground, and declare victory. Being your child's parent is the role of a lifetime and you were meant to play it. As long as you contend that you are a parent by accident, you leave room to give yourself a "pass," and can choose to check out. But making that choice won't be good for you

> *Know that you were hand-picked by God, chosen for your role in your family's story.*

or your child. So even if you're not ready to settle the matter of being "chosen" or "called" to be a parent (much less prepared), you will be far more likely to actually become a positive parent if you move forward at least with the hope and belief that maybe, just maybe you were born for this.

No matter how ill-prepared you may feel, know that you are not an accidental parent, and your child is not an accident either. Anyone can become a great parent. Like any behavior, it is learned, and therefore it can be re-learned, modified, and improved. Would you expect yourself to dance perfectly the first time you tried it? Neither can you expect to parent without the mishaps and blunders that go along with learning how to navigate something new and different.

In general, you will parent the way you were parented, unless you make a personal, lasting decision to do better. Your children are given to you for a number of years so that you can help guide and point them in the direction that they should go. It's a noble responsibility—but you're up for it.

YOUR CHILD IS HERE BY DESIGN

Jim Collin's 2001 bestseller, *Good to Great,* analyzes companies that research has indicated are the most successful. Without exception, these companies did not come to that success by accident, but rather by design. Corporate success stories are inevitably populated by heroes that had a clear purpose and mission. Furthermore, their top management excelled at communicating that purpose, vision, and mission to the employees. Everyone was on the same page and took pride in knowing they were not just working, they were working for something.

Parents who say "I'm just not cut out for this" cannot hope for success. When things are going wrong, it's easy to question whether you have the chops for parenting at all, let alone parenting well. Maybe your doubts stem from a teenage daughter who is going through serious rebellion issues—she's running with the wrong crowd, getting involved in drugs, or threatening to move out of the house and in with her boyfriend who lives in a van down by the river. You can almost hear the insidious whisper in your ear: "It must be your fault; you're just not cut out to be the parent of a teenager."

I remember sitting with an adopted teenager who was coming to grips with his unique family makeup. His eyes lit up as he said that he realized that he was supposed to be in his adoptive family, it is where he belonged and he was placed there and was chosen. His perspective that life was purposeful and not random gave him a great sense of confidence. Approaching your roles as a parent with the assurance that this is part of your purpose, your "mission" in life will help you as a parent.

Believing in a purpose and design foster greater conviction to stay engaged no matter how difficult, depressing, or heartbreaking the circumstances may be at the moment.

In most good stories there is a point where the hero cannot turn back: Frodo from the Lord of the Rings realizes that the burden of the ring is his to carry; Marvel Comics' Iron Man decides that the only way to save the country is by sacrificing himself. This is also true in life. When early settlers came to America, they would often burn their ships once they reached their destination so there could be no way to back out of their commitment. Realize that you are the parent and that there is no one else that can complete your specific task, and get to work.

> *Believing in a purpose and design foster greater conviction to stay engaged no matter how difficult, depressing, or heartbreaking the circumstances may be at the moment.*

As you look at your own family story, don't feel discouraged if the past or current story is not what you envision for your family. This might be why you are reading this book right now, to make some course corrections and influence the future storyline to become a gripping tale for future generations to come. It doesn't have to be a far-off fairytale; it can become your reality.

Chapter 2

Shaping a Great Family Story

"I WISH MY KIDS CAME WITH AN OWNER'S MANUAL!"

I ATTENDED A 2-DAY workshop on how to write a great story. The auditorium was filled with eager young writers and Hollywood types all wanting to know how to craft the next big blockbuster. The speaker, who had been advertised as the guy people hire to fix lackluster screenplays responded to the question by saying there is no formula for a great story, only principles. So how do you write a better story for your family? Here are six principles that can be used in shaping a great family story.

#1—Create High Emotional Warmth

We have all seen movies or read books with epic action: crashing cars, searing lasers, and flying fists keep our attention for the duration of the scene. A story that is full of action must also have warmth—a plot or sub-plot with some emotional connectedness. We often read reviews of the latest action film where there is high intensity and conflict but the characters are basically static; they are not moving in any particular direction. There seems to be no warmth or emotional direction. Despite the hype, those movies usually fail to reach blockbuster status.

A good family story must also possess a degree of warmth. If there is very little warmth among the characters, the movie will lack compelling movement. By warmth, I am not implying that everyone should constantly enjoy and invite the presence of other family members or that families should cross over the balance from healthy to enmeshed, but there must be some overt positive emotion displayed on a frequent basis among all members. Events as simple as snuggling on the couch with popcorn for family movie night, playing ball together, or kind conversations shared over a meal evoke warmth and fondness in a family. Do your spouse and children know that you love them, not only by words, but by your presence, conversations, and demeanor? Does your daughter know that when she has a broken heart that you will actually listen, or would she assume you will tell her to "suck it up" and get over it? Does your family know the difference between laughing together at a funny event rather than laughing at one another? Screen writers have a name for adding warmth to a movie. They call it "saving the cat." If the hero does not "save the cat" early in the story, the audience is not compelled to pull for him. There is usually a vulnerable moment with the hero within the first 15 minutes of a movie.

#2—Have Low and Productive Conflict

Is your family story one of conflict? We all deal with conflict, and conflict is not always bad. Benjamin Franklin said, "Those things that hurt, instruct." Our children need to see conflicts resolved, problems remedied, and bad circumstances mitigated. The research of Drs. John and Julie Gottman at the Gottman Institute has revealed that longevity in marriage can be predicted by the couple's ability to resolve conflict. The same is true in creating a wholesome, healthy family unit. Is your family currently bogged down in conflict? If so, this unresolved conflict can damage the relationships in the family. Addressing these issues can not only restore relationships, but also teach important life skills. The solution may be found in something as simple as a family meeting and consensus, or it may require going to a counselor.

#3 - Have High Fun

Having fun with the family is often much easier said than done, or planned than accomplished. The best fun is spontaneous, but life doesn't always create situations that are fun for the entire family in a singular moment. If your family is succeeding in having low conflict and high warmth, the fun will come more naturally. That said, there are proactive steps that you can take to create windows of opportunity. For example, if you tell your kids that there can be no internet, video or phone for one hour each evening (or one or two evenings per week) that might allow time for a board game or a walk around the neighborhood. What about pretending that you are visitors to your town and discovering what the "tourists" do when visiting your city? In a good story, conflict is often momentarily put aside for some comedic relief. It can allow the viewer to relax, enjoy the story line, and give a more complete perspective of the situation. Laughter creates emotional bonds, loosens tensions and the investments in time will greatly enhance the relationships in your home.

#4—Have High Purpose or Theme

All the best stories have an underlining purpose or theme running through them. The details of the plot are held together by this cosmic cause or purpose that pulls the characters through the story. What's your family about? If a friend or neighbor was asked to describe your family, what would they say? Would they describe your family as athletic, compassionate, scholarly, dysfunctional, laden with addictions, or wild? How would you like to be described as a family? To know how to write the rest of the story, take a look how your family operates now. What is the theme of your family story so far? To find the answer analyze your story to date. One of the basic premises of behavior theory is that one will eventually become only what they are becoming today. Decide what you want the theme or purpose of your family life to be. Depending upon the ages of your children, you might want to involve them in the discussion. Create a family motto, a goal. Creating a sense of family identity is important and meaningful.

The movie *The Blind Side* told the story of the Tuohy family who adopted a young man of a different race and helped him to succeed in life. The movie described the family's wealth, love for their alma mater, and the personalities of the different family members. But it was a great story because it had a compelling theme. Several times in the movie, Mrs. Tuohy would answer questions about why they were helping Michael Oher by simply responding, "You do what is the right thing to do." The Tuohy's are a family who, when presented with a situation that pushed them out of their comfort zone, chose to do what they considered the right thing to do because that is how they define their family narrative.

Take time to identify the theme or purpose for your family. Not only will it help your kids to feel like there is meaning and reason for being connected beyond just living and surviving, it will likely generate deeper ties to each other, creating more emotional warmth into your family storyline. What will be the theme of your family?

#5—Answer the Right Question

Children are continually asking two basic questions: "Am I loved?" and "Can I do this without suffering negative consequences?" The first question concerns love, the second concerns boundaries and structure. It seems as if most parents are good at answering only one of these questions. For example, if a daughter asks her mom, "Do you think I can become the president?", to which the mom answers, "Well, Honey, you would need to study hard and get good grades in school if you want to become the president," she, the mom is answering the wrong question. The daughter is asking, "Am I loved? Do you believe in me?" The mom did answer the second question of "Can I do this?" by describing what it takes and what the requirements would consist of to pursue her dream of becoming the president.

I would like to invite you into the tension of boldly answering both of these questions. Just be clear about which question is really being asked.

#6—Parent Consistently

I love to watch small children as they learn the precarious movements of locomotion. Their walking often looks more like an unsuccessful fall than a successful walk, yet somehow they learn. We have small grandchildren now and it's a blast watching them wiggle and struggle with first learning how to roll over, then scooch across the floor, to finally pulling themselves up to end tables and couch fronts. Then the magical day arrives when they venture out, first one hand off, then the second. They teeter a bit and take that first step. A toddler learns to walk due to the consistency of gravity. If she leans over too far in either direction, a fall is inevitable. That consistent feedback teaches the child to walk and run, and eventually they can navigate the world. As parents, we need to strive towards providing our children with a level of consistency that will not only help them feel safe but help them learn and grow.

In telling a great story, what makes a character believable is consistency in their behavior. People are wired in certain ways and act accordingly. So when someone does something distinctly out of character, people notice. If they deviate out of character too often, it becomes unbelievable. An important principle of positive parenting is consistency. Consistency builds trust and trust is an essential building block of a healthy family.

As a kid growing up in the Midwest, whenever my dad came home from work, he would check my room. If my bed wasn't made correctly, he would immediately call me in from play and marshal me upstairs to remake my bed properly. It irritated me, but it was just the rule of the house. The bed had to be made, and made correctly, each day. (This meant hospital corners, lines on the bedspread straight, and the bottom edge hanging about one inch from the floor.) I never realized how much effort it took for my parents to enforce this rule... not until I became a parent. As an adult, when I come home from work, the last thing I want to be is the bad guy, making my kids pause their video games or whatever they are doing to come in and make a bed.

When you come home tired or you have been working with your child at home throughout the day, there comes a point when you desire some peace and rest. You do not want to hold your child accountable for tasks either undone or incorrectly completed. No one wants to listen to the whining and complaining, and then wait for them to redo or properly complete the task the second time around. But it is important to consistently enforce your household rules. Parenting is work—it's a job, a career, and it demands dedicated and consistent effort.

The principle here is clearly not about making beds. I personally don't care whether your kids make their beds every day or not. (Truthfully, no one in our home has to make his or her bed.) But once you make a rule, any rule of the house, you must be prepared to consistently enforce and reinforce it. Kids are desperate for consistency in their lives, and as the parent, you have a major responsibility for creating consistency and stability in your home. You can't consistently enforce the rules of your home without some sort of discipline measures to back up those rules. Discipline is really just training or teaching tactics and should not be viewed as punishment—but we'll talk more about discipline later on.

Consistency Makes the Difference

Children spend less time watching television and playing video games if their parents are consistent about the limits they set on screen time and insist that they get exercise, a new study found. . . . Based on such findings, the American Academy of Pediatrics recommends that parents limit total screen media time for children older than two to no more than two hours of quality programming a day. "However, it is not just the presence or absence of rules that is important but also the consistency of the rules and whether children and adolescents are aware of the rules."[1]

Choose your rules carefully, and agree with your partner about what is most important. Whether the rule is about doing your homework before you watch TV or taking your shoes off before you enter the house, it's critical that the enforcement of your rule is applied consistently every time.

In modern life, rules seemingly change quickly, and sometimes just for the sake of convenience. This can actually be profoundly disturbing to kids. Kids long for consistency in their lives, and despite the hassle or inconvenience of it, having reasonable rules, knowing the rules and having them enforced consistently is essential to creating a safe and positive home environment.

---

[1] Susan A. Carlson, MPH and colleagues of the Centers for Disease Control and Prevention.

CONSISTENT EXPECTATIONS

However, consistency is not just about enforcing rules. It's also about how we react to the unplanned moments of life. Perhaps Mom will get all flustered and bent out of shape over that spilled sippy cup of juice on one occasion, but then the next time it happens she acts as if it's no big deal. What is a kid to think of the Dad who one time shrugs his shoulders over a broken curfew, but the next time goes ballistic? Kids will become insecure when they don't know what to expect from us. This is why when we parent, we mustn't operate out of our emotions—our emotions are generally not consistent. We must operate out of principal and not convenience.

On the other hand, parents should not be emotionless robots either. Children can interpret a parent's controlling his or her emotions as not caring. We must show our emotions, particularly through love. Balance is the key, not stoicism. We can express positive emotions through regular hugs, smiles, and encouragement, as well as reasonable displeasure by way of a quick but fair rebuke. The key is, we must never lose control of our emotions, especially when disciplining a child for misconduct. In fact, when parents become truly angry, they should take their own "time out" to collect their wits before administering discipline, be it corporal punishment, grounding, or loss of privileges. Taking time to collect those wits can help parents avoid extremes that they may find themselves regretting later.

Kids are desperate for consistency in their lives.

I'm speaking from experience. Occasionally one of my children will do something to irritate me. For the sake of discussion, let's say my son either ignores my request or manages to muster an almost inaudible grunt as a response to a question. Even though my normal response nine out of ten times is measured, if I lose control and blow up at him on that particular day when I'm already frustrated about something, I'm not being consistent. I am teaching him by example that I can't be trusted. He never knows for sure which Dad is going to react to him: Dr. Jekyll or Mr. Hyde. When this happens (and if human blood runs through your veins, trust me, you will blow it from time to time), be quick to recognize your inconsistency or overreaction. Pull back. If necessary, apologize.

Consistency also brings security into children's lives by way of boundaries. Parents can easily fall into the trap of setting inconsistent boundaries, which is an accident waiting to happen. There are two sides to any good boundary: expectations and consequences. Both sides need our best efforts. Inconsistent boundaries place children in a "no-win" situation. If on the one hand we verbalize consequences, but fail to follow through with action, children will become confused and insecure, often developing poor behavior habits. They'll figure out all too quickly that "no" doesn't really mean no—at least not until the fourth time you say it. But clear expectations and consequences enhance children's chances of success.

Children really do want to please their parents, believe it or not. They feel more secure in being loved when we set consistent boundaries and give them the chance to honor us through obedience. This is not mere rules-for-rules'-sake legalism. What I am suggesting is you need to consistently give your child clear enough information so he or she has the opportunity to honor you. In order to help ensure your child's success, you need to help him or her obey. Along with consistent rules, let your love for your kids stay consistent as well. They want to know you will be there for them no matter what and that your love for them is not conditional on their behavior. This is a hard balancing act that nobody can master easily, but is important to the health and well-being of your family relationship.

Consistency counts!

CONSISTENT CONSEQUENCES

The other side of the consistent-boundaries equation is consequence. Parents may do very well with setting expectations, but they can still fail to set or deliver consequences. By this I mean both what we consider negative as well as positive consequences.

Consistency in consequences is one of the most important lessons your children can learn. If there are little or ineffectual consequences in the home, children struggle. They learn nothing about discipline and don't understand the "real world" of consequences they will face as adults. It's always someone else's fault or responsibility. Poor parenting in this area has terrible consequences, not only for your child but for our communities, our culture, and our world. Consequences are designed to foster discipline by rewarding good behavior, giving additional instruction, and providing motivation to correct bad choices.

But clear expectations and consequences enhance children's chances of success.

Be consistent in giving positive consequences as well. Few things are worse than loving someone who you feel you can never please. It seems like no matter what you do, it's never enough. That's not a healthy way for children or adults to feel. If your child did what you asked, tell them thanks and let them know how much you appreciate their help. Even if they didn't give it their best effort, find something positive in what they did. If the forks ended up on the wrong side of the plate when you asked them to set the table, so what? Praise your child for helping to set the table. If they need additional instruction, give it in a loving way. Perhaps next time, you can explain that while there's really not a right or wrong way to set the table, our culture generally places the forks on the left side of the plate. Practice what I call the "Yes, and" principle. Instead of saying, "No, you didn't set the table correctly," try saying, "Yes, thank you for setting the table; and next time, let's put the fork over on the left side of the plate. That way you are doing it just like all the fanciest restaurants do it."

Expect your children to contribute to the family work and take on increasing levels of responsibility. That's also a form of consistency. It may seem a whole lot easier to just do things yourself, but you are doing what's best for your children when you involve them in family responsibilities. So look past the complaining. And consistently find reasons to give them verbal rewards that are appropriate, frequent, and sincere.

FAILURE TO FOLLOW THROUGH

What if you asked your child to set the table and they fail to do so? Do you set the table for them and ignore their disobedience? Do you rant and rave about how no one ever listens to you? Do you make sure they heard you and gently remind them that you need their help? Do you apologize for interrupting their video game or TV show? Just how far can they go before they push your button? Is the child controlling the parent or is the parent parenting the child?

When it comes to power struggles and discipline, consistency counts. Your child needs to know you will consistently stay in control of yourself and the situation while gently yet firmly guiding him or her toward obedience and the desired behavior. Otherwise, children figure out how to play us against ourselves and get what they want, even when it's not what's best for them. If you give children a path of least resistance, they will take it almost every time. Consistency counts. Much like that regular oil change your car needs, it's "pay me now or pay me later." It is much easier to deliver consistent consequences when children are young than to begin being consistent during the teen years. If you weren't consistent with them from an early age, it becomes increasingly difficult (though not impossible) to set the boundaries.

We said earlier that what makes a great character in a story is consistency. Likewise, being consistent in the way we handle our children and their actions will help build *their* character and tell a better story.

Section Two

Reflecting—
Character

Chapter 3

Follow Me

"I JUST DON'T WANT MY KIDS TO MAKE THE SAME MISTAKES I DID."

C RAP, CRAP, CRAP, holy crap!" Our son Skylar's voice was being broadcast over the airwaves for all of Central Florida to hear. One of the traits of autism is that ideas can become "stuck" in one's mind. The previous evening he had been watching a rerun of "Everybody Loves Raymond." In the sitcom, the occasionally abrasive and often socially inappropriate father often says, "Holy Crap." My wife was the seventh caller into a local radio station whose tagline is "Always Safe for the Little Ears." When the radio host told my wife she had just won a set of tickets to Disney, Skylar became excited and started yelling the first phrase that came into his mind. Later that day, friends called and told us how funny it was to hear him in the background. We now have the distinction of violating the "Safe for the Little Ears" tagline. We did not teach Skye that phrase, but it was introduced to him on TV. Our children are like sponges, constantly absorbing information from their environment.

Like a good story, a family is made of well-developed characters. We have all seen the movie that leaves us disappointed because characters were not well developed. In this section, we will use the idea of "reflecting" to speak about the development of the family story. The characters within a family story are shaped by the reflections of the dominant members of the family, which is usually you, the parent. Parents are responsible for modeling appropriate and desirable behavior as well as being intentional about how the children are developing. Your children will tend to "reflect" what they have seen and learned from you. Who you are as a person, how you live, how you handle difficulty and stress, and how well you love others will be far more influential and compelling for your child than any lesson you try to teach them.

It may seem a whole lot easier to just do things yourself, but you are doing what's best for your children when you involve them in family responsibilities.

In the classic study by Bandura, children were shown violent cartoons and observed at play. They proved what all grandmothers know, that we learn by modeling. As vicarious learners, we copy what we see. The old admonition to "do as I say, not as I do" may sound catchy but simply is not true. The values

we hold, our priorities in life, the things we believe, the lifestyle
habits we embrace are more "caught" than "taught."

Kids watch you. It's scary to realize how much they do. There
was a classic TV commercial against smoking that showed
a dad and a young son together. The son was watching and
copying the dad's actions, imitating him as he shaved, as he
mowed the lawn. It was heartwarming, right down to the point
where the dad pulled a pack of cigarettes out of his pocket and
lit up. Nothing needed to be said. Viewers of the commercial
got the message loud and clear.

Each character in the play must be willing to accept the fact
that they impact the other characters, especially the members
that are cast as parents and guardians. What are you teaching
your kids by example that you do not want them to emulate?

My father was a workaholic, and although I was never told
that was the way that a man should be, it is what I became. As
I look at the landscape of my life and see some of the choices
that I have made due to this tendency to
overwork, I am sad to know that my children have now watched me live this way.
A person's greatest fear should not be that
they will fail, because we will all fail at
times. Your greatest fear should be that
you will succeed at something that does

*What are you
teaching your kids
by example that
you do not want
them to emulate?*

not matter. Have I taught my children to succeed at things that
do not matter? It is inevitable our children will follow some of
our examples.

This truth that values are caught and not taught was ham-
mered home to me at an education conference that I hosted several years ago. The riveting words, "Until you can say, 'follow

me,' you've got nothing to say," were spoken by one of our key-note speakers. She was a young woman whose parents were missionaries in Columbia. Local drug lords had marked their family for death. The audience was held in rapt attention as this young woman detailed the miraculous events that kept her family safe from harm even as they were living in the local community attempting to love and serve its people. The speaker explained that learning to trust God for her provision and safety was something she learned through that trying experience that enabled her to authentically share with the local residents that they too could trust God.

A person's greatest fear should not be that they will fail, because we will all fail at times. Your greatest fear should be that you will succeed at something that does not matter.

That simple phrase, "Until you can say 'follow me', you've got nothing to say," has left a great impression on me—especially as I think about my role as a parent. Am I living a life that I would want my children to follow? I'm not saying my kids have to emulate what I do for a living, or enjoy the same hobbies, interests, or sports. What I am saying is that one of the most powerful parenting truths you can embrace is to simply live in a way you would want your children to follow. This one truth has great power in the family story. When you fully realize that you are the one that they are following, your desire will become to write the greatest family story possible.

EYES ARE WATCHING YOU

Politicians, coaches, generals, and parents all have the incredible privilege and responsibility of leading others. Teams take on the personality of their coaches, organizations adopt the personality of their leader, and children mirror the modeled behavior of their parents. It is difficult for a story to live beyond the depth of the main characters.

It is often said that imitation is the sincerest form of flattery. This saying rings true. Your children watch you. You are their source of comfort and credibility. You are the norm that they intuitively understand that they are to follow. Even if you have a child who is particularly independent and rebellious, you still establish clear patterns of behavior and thinking. Scary isn't it? We don't really want that responsibility, do we? We send our kids off to school, to camp, to Sunday school, and to summer jobs in the hope that someone else will be a strong role model, a strong example for them to follow. But the fact remains that you are the single most influential role model for the majority of your child's maturing years. All too quickly your children will become more aware and open to adopting the values and behavior of their peers and what they see on TV. Make sure that for the most crucial and formative years of their life, they adopt their core values from you. Remember that they will stay interested in the family if the story the family is writing is compelling.

Children do not acquire the ability to reason abstractly until late in their teen years. The themes, attitudes, behaviors, and examples they grow up with become their norm. As a parent, you get to define "normal." You teach about gender, relationships, conflict, self-soothing, work ethic, social behavior and how to deal with emotions. These become deeply engrained values, beliefs, and norms. Even in the teen years when children begin to question, argue, and think more independently (a natural and positive progression), the way that you talk and walk, how you respond to adversity, and how you respond to your child all contribute to his or her training. It's a heavy burden, without doubt. You are the primary teacher and example for your child. Nobody else can, or should be the main character in your family story. As a parent, you want to live with reasonable mental, emotional and physical health, not just for you but for your children. If you are not in a place of basic mental health, it's completely appropriate to ask for some outside help.

> **Self-Soothing Behavior**
>
> The Gottman's have conducted excellent research on how to parent emotionally intelligent children. For more information, go to: https://www.gottman.com/shop/raising-an-emotionally-intelligent-child-the-heart-of-parenting-book/.

This is not a call to be perfect. As a matter of fact, some of my best parenting has been when I have had to deal directly with my children about some of my parenting mistakes. Remember that the main character of a good story is not a character without flaws, but is a dynamic character that grows and changes with the movement of the story. One of our responsibilities is to allow our children to watch us navigate the twists and turns of life so that they will eventually write their own great story.

Don't Forget Your Supporting Cast

We no longer live in the 1950's when the streets, the movies and most family goals were black and white; when Mom wore an apron and Dad only came into the story on the weekends. Our world now has more opportunities, but also a lot more temptations. It is much messier now. You are not alone in this process; you can seek out and help your children find other positive role models.

I am not an outdoorsman, but my youngest son loves the smell of leaves, the snap of twigs as he listens for prey, and the smell of freshly cleaned fish over a fire. In my attempt to bond with him I have worn the camo uniform, been stung by paintballs, slept on rocks that masqueraded as earth, and prayed that a deer would not approach as we crouched in a deer stand. I threw up in the ocean when I tried to surf and ran out of oxygen while scuba diving with him. We have tried our best to encourage him and

> You are the single most influential role model for the majority of your child's maturing years.

support his interests, and it was important that I participate in his passions. It was obvious to my son that my desire was to be with him, not necessarily to participate in the activities.

While I was teaching at a small college in Tennessee, a student of mine named Andrew was an avid outdoorsman. Once I knew him well enough to trust him, I introduced him to my son. Decades later, Samuel counts Andrew as one of his best friends. Even though the parental role is crucial, it is important for your children to have supporting characters, other models in their lives. I'm extremely grateful for the many positive influences that have impacted my own children. Conversely, if you see your son or daughter making unwise choices in the friends they are choosing to follow and emulate, don't take a passive stance in this area. Get involved enough to know when you may need to step in and make some hard choices about limiting your child's interaction with negative role models. We'll talk more about this in the "Protecting" section of this book.

It's important to surround your child with a variety of people who positively model for them how to think and respond in life. Just remember that the primary responsibility for shaping your child's story and your family story remains with you as the parent. You don't need a college education or a unique set of skills and experiences to teach your child how to live and behave well. You just need to *be* a person who lives and behaves well.

Parents More Influential Than Teachers

Students in Georgia who participated in a recent survey overwhelmingly agree that it is their parents—not their teachers, not their coaches or religious leaders, not their peers, not the celebrities they are enamored with at the moment—who are the biggest influencers as to how well they do in school. More than six hundred high school students from four diverse regions of Georgia were surveyed.[2]

What You Pass Along—Legacy

History repeats itself. Family dynamics repeat themselves. Some of this may be genetic, some may be learned. Scientists are still debating the subject. Part of being a reflective parent is to examine your own family history to see how it has influenced the way that you parent. There are rules and vows in each family.

My father was old school. My dad made it clear that we could never wear a hat to the dinner table and that a shirt was worn at all times. I am not sure that I ever decided that it was an important rule, I probably never did. His rules became a way for me to understand and measure life. We tend to not question rules that we have experienced our entire lives. When I moved my family to Florida it became my son's job to mow the grass. One day during ninety-five degree heat and stifling humidity he walked into our home without a shirt on after mowing. I told him that he must put a shirt on, and he looked at me incredulously as I uttered the proclamation, "Coffield men wear shirts." I heard my father's voice as I repeated this arbitrary rule. This rule was quickly and summarily suspended.

What rules, patterns and values did you inherit? Some rules can have more serious implications than my dad's "shirt rule." Some of the rules we inherit should be examined. For example, "Big boys don't cry," "What goes on in our home is private," or "Never say 'I'm sorry'," might need to be reconsidered. Think of all the rules that are just accepted as normal

---

[2] PR Newswire, "Georgia Students Rank Parents as Primary Influencers in School Success," news release, November 29, 2005, http://www.prnewswire.com/news-releases/georgia-students-rank-parents-as-primary-influencers-in-school-success-55732737.html.

even though they are silly or don't make sense to the present situation or culture. These "rules" are really just learned behaviors that have been ingrained in our cultures, but they can be chosen and changed.

Other rules we inherited from our childhood can positively help shape our character and might indeed want to be passed on. To this day, I can still hear my dad saying to me: "If it's worth doing, it's worth doing right." That rule of doing things with excellence has stuck with me long past my childhood. It is important to reflect upon the rules you grew up with and decide which rules you will keep and which ones are arbitrary or don't line up with your values. However, if you do not reflect upon the rules and values you inherited, you will find yourself parroting rules from your childhood that may no longer be helpful or relevant.

More important than the rules, are the vows that you have made while growing up. A vow is simply a promise that we make to do something. Vows are often made as the result of difficult times or great successes. We will

If you can't say, "Follow me," you've got nothing to say.

make deep commitments and vows, such as, "I will never be embarrassed like that again," or "I will never let anyone hurt me like that again," or "I will win at any cost." The vows that we make to never be alone, embarrassed, caught, poor, etc., are vows that drive our behaviors.

My wife grew up in a large family with financial struggles. Her family used plastic dining when she was young. Most likely, they did this because there were five children and it simply made sense. But in her mind, eating from plastic plates indicated that they were poor. Decades later, when we were making choices for our wedding registry, she told me that our family would never eat from plastic plates. She had made a silent vow as a child that her children would never feel as if they were poor; therefore, they would always eat from china, pottery, or glass. The rules we choose to uphold along with the vows we take, shape our identity.

Later, we will talk about building your child's identity, but you must be aware of what has shaped your own. A reflective parent will reflect upon what has shaped their own identity and how that has, in turn, shaped their parenting. There is danger in continuing to allow your identity to be defined by your past. If we want to rewrite our story, we must stop behaviors we don't want our children to copy. It is not as simple as saying, "stop." Most likely you will need to examine your own family of origin. By facing the vows and rules reflected upon you, you will be able to choose which parts of your history to pass on to your children. Without an honest look inward, you will inadvertently pass on old rules, old legacies, and old hurts. You will be requiring your sons to wear shirts at all times, and not even understand why.

DOING IT FOR THE KIDS

When I was growing up, both my parents smoked cigarettes. My mom gave up smoking when I was a teenager, but my dad had a harder time quitting. He tried a few times but never succeeded. Then one Christmas, when my wife Amy and I announced that Amy was pregnant, and we were going to have our first child, my father responded by saying, "My grandchild will never see me smoke." That was important to him. He was living for someone besides himself. He didn't have the will-power or motivation to quit smoking just for himself, but he didn't want his future grandson or granddaughter to see him smoke. He didn't want to set that example for them.

So my question to you is this: What are the things in your life that you wouldn't want to see your child (or children) emulate? What are the habits and attitudes that you wouldn't wish on your kids? After all, if you can't say, "Follow me," you've got nothing to say.

We live in a time where people do not like to accept personal responsibility for their actions. If we lose our temper at home it's because of the stress at work. It's much easier to offer an excuse than to change our behavior. We pop pills like we're munching on peanuts. We spend millions, maybe billions of dollars annually on therapy sessions and counseling all because we had a bad childhood...and then we live out the same model in front of our own kids.

Be the person who says, "The destructive behavior stops with me." You may come from a long line of alcohol abusers; maybe your father had a horrible temper and so do you. But for the sake of your kids and future generations of your family, choose to work through these patterns and resolve, "It stops with me. I will not pass on the heritage of negative behavior to the next generation." Because as long as you can't say to your child, "Follow me" . . . well, you get my point.

Chapter 4

Storyboard Principles— Family Values

"I CAN'T BELIEVE I SOUND JUST LIKE MY PARENTS"

WHEN WRITERS COME together, they often create a story-board that shows the movement of the story. Much like this, our values help us create our own storyboard and emphasize those characteristics that are important to us. If you value cooperation more than competition, it will impact the way you conduct your life and how you parent your children.

"During a question and answer time after a parenting seminar, a man asked, "We just had a newborn. When will the child be able to remember what I do and don't do, so that I will know when I must become involved?" To begin with, I was a little concerned for his wife and child. He was asking the wrong question. The basic understanding of love, trust, and personality are established at early ages. So while the infant may not cognitively understand what she experiences, she is profoundly affected by what is experienced in the home. The key concept here that I don't want you to miss is that you reflect to your child not so much what you teach but who you are. Your values, both stated and hidden, will be lived out and demonstrated in both obvious and subtle ways throughout your child's growing up years, and it will have a profound impact on them. So be sure to reflect the values and priorities you want your children to capture.

While he or she may not have the cognitive capacity or education to articulate beliefs and attitudes, a young child's values are being significantly established very early on by what they observe and experience at home.

Parents need to purposefully decide the themes—the values of the family. If these values are not purposefully chosen, the influences of media, peers, and old habits will establish them by default.

What are the values you are teaching... or perhaps more accurately, what are the values you are reflecting? What is scrawled atop your storyboard? **What are the themes running through your story? What are your values?**

Parents need to purposefully decide the themes—the values of the family. If these values are not purposefully chosen, the influences of media, peers, and old habits will establish them by default. If you will take time to reflect and determine the core themes and values you want your children to embrace, and strive to be consistent in living your own life by those values, you will be more likely to create a positive family story.

My wife once ran a preschool. It is interesting to see how zealous preschool moms can be when it comes to making sure that their child is getting as much intellectual stimulation as possible. We all want our children to get ahead—to have an edge in school and in life. We often erroneously believe that the brightest come out on top, but that is not necessarily true.

The world doesn't belong to the smartest. It belongs to the brave, the noble, and the compassionate. So relax, kindergarten is not a race. It's not even so much about acquiring foundational information. It's a starting point for the love of learning, the art of interacting with others, and the realization that we are here to serve others instead of ourselves. As parents, we can spend too much time worrying about our children's education, while neglecting their internal values. The early years are the best times to form our children's character so they become balanced, secure, confident people—people who can take risks because they are not afraid of failure. The values we teach our young children are not learned through worksheets and grades. Our children learn the values, themes, and purpose of their story by what we reflect to them.

THE HEART OF YOUR FAMILY

There was a nationwide study done a few years ago that revealed that most lifelong beliefs are formed by the age of twelve.[3]

---

[3] George Barna, *Transforming Children into Spiritual Champions* (Ventura, CA: Gospel Light, 2003), 22.

If the prevailing worldview in your household is materialistic, if shopping is considered an art form, and success is measured by what you have rather than who you are, you are setting a theme, a value that possessions are more important than people. As I have gotten older, I recognize I am still influenced and impacted by the values I inherited from my father. He was a good father and for that I am grateful. But, good or bad, I see so clearly the influences of my family upbringing throughout my adult life. I had lunch recently with a friend who shared how he is struggling with the tension of being available for his family versus being consumed with his work. It didn't take more than a few minutes to learn that as a child his family went from relative financial security to insecurity because of the failure of his father's business. My friend suddenly began to realize how his own fears and desire for financial security were motivating him to overwork. Clearly the values and environment you reflect to your children have lasting implications.

So what are the values that you wish to bestow upon your children? We can all make a list of negative attitudes and values that we don't want them to have. That's a long but easy list to make. But what values do you "own" or would like to own? Let me suggest three core values as a starting point as you carve out the not-so-hidden curriculum of your family.

#1—Your Children Have Great Worth—They Are Sacred

We are obsessed with attempting to make our children feel special, although deep inside we realize that as spectacular as human beings are, most of us are ordinary. Instead of trying to teach your child to feel special, let me suggest another word to use—sacred. Sacredness is a foundational value. It is a precept upon which the way that you treat others is based. Sacredness is not earned, it is declared and bestowed. The ground of Gettysburg battlefield is no longer an ordinary meadow. It is a sacred place, declared sacred by the blood that was shed. Life will teach your child that most of us are ordinary; very few become president of the United States, most of us are not valedictorians, and astronauts have become an exceedingly rare group of individuals. Yet, when your child begins to doubt their significance and worth, they can be encouraged by the knowledge that they have a value and dignity that is not related to their performance, physical attributes, or talents.

Clearly the values and environment you reflect to your children have lasting implications.

Ironically, it is my son with special needs who taught me this. On paper, he offers very little to society, and might even be viewed by some as a burden. I consider his life as valuable as anyone else's. His dreams and hopes, though limited, are the dreams and hopes of a man. When children are treated as if they are valued and sacred, they grow up exhibiting grace and dignity rather than depravity and despair. Children will often learn how greatly they are valued when they experience their greatest failures.

Ultimately, it is easy for a child to feel your love when they perceive that you are pleased with them. It is often within the rocky soil of failure that the reality of sacredness is planted. I remember an especially difficult conversation that I had with one of my children as she approached the age of twenty-one. I was not pleased with the choices or the direction that she was choosing in life. As a result, there were consequences that she would be facing. "Rachel, no matter what you do, you will always be my beloved daughter." With tears in both of our eyes, we realized that something sacred had occurred. I explained to her that there was absolutely nothing that she could do to ever diminish my love for her or our family, but that I would not financially facilitate her choices or prevent her consequences. It is important that your child know that you have the faith in them to believe that they can deal with the natural consequences of their choices.

The most unproductive person has more intrinsic value than the most productive computer or machine; what makes us individuals who can love unconditionally is irreproducible and beyond human invention—the soul cannot be artificially manufactured. For instance, preschool children don't normally contribute to society. Their value stems simply from the fact that they are people—they were created. They are valued and loved. You as the parent are the primary way they learn to embrace that they are loved and have worth.

When your child begins to doubt their significance and worth, they can be encouraged by the knowledge that they have a value and dignity that is not related to their performance, physical attributes, or talents.

When a child truly feels valued, they will develop a positive self-image. It is a priceless gift from a parent that is bestowed by believing in and practicing unconditional love or sacredness. At this point in my life I have spent countless hours as a counselor across the couch while people speak about their lives. One of the most common disappointments that I hear is, "I wish my parents told me they loved me more often," or, "I wish my dad was proud of me." Save your children the couch time later and live the theme of unconditional worth in your home. Giving your child the gift of a positive self-image is one of the most powerful, amazing, and important values you can ever impart.

Our sense of self-worth must be based not on our achievement but on our birthright. If self-worth was born from achievement, star athletes, actors, millionaires, and business moguls would have high self-esteem and the rest of us would struggle with feelings of inadequacy. But we have all read stories of the rich and famous who struggle mightily with their self-esteem and conversely, of those who barely subsist on meager wages but are able to live contented lives surrounded by loved ones.

The Power of Genuine Praise

As parents, we shouldn't underestimate the power of our words and the impact of our genuine praise on our children.

Alice, now a mother of two, says, "I remember how my mother used to talk about my beautiful red hair. Her positive comments as she combed my hair before school have been a constant part of my self-perception. Years later when I discovered that we redheads are in the minority, I never had negative feelings about my red hair. I'm sure my mother's loving comments had a lot to do with that."

When you want to build up your child's self-esteem by words of praise, take the following tips into account in order to make your words effective.

1. Don't be careless and give vague comments, like, "You are a good boy or a good girl." It works for younger children, but not for older ones, teens, or grownups.

2. Careless praises used too frequently will have little effect.

3. The words have to both be true and justified.
    Without any genuine expression, they'll regard it
    as flattery, or worse, a lie.

4. Know how to handle your own emotions appro-
    priately and maturely, especially in frustration
    or anger. No encouraging message would come
    out from our mouths when we are still struggling
    with our emotions, even though we think we are
    saying some correct words.

5. Learn how to speak softly and pleasantly.

6. Use questions whenever possible, rather than
    issuing commands. Rather than demanding, "Do
    this now," try asking, "I'd like to have your help—
    would you do this for me?" Using questions will
    bring better responses from older children espe-
    cially.

7. Learn to catch your child being or doing good,
    and then commend him or her for it. Then your
    words would not be vague, but substantial instead.
    For example, "When you shared your toys with
    Bob, I felt very proud of you because you are very
    considerate."

8. Go for guidance, rather than mere dos and don'ts.
    Simply demanding "don't smoke" or "don't get
    pregnant" or "don't experiment with drugs" or
    "don't exceed the speed limit" may all be well
    intentioned warnings, but they are hardly enough
    guidance to develop a meaningful life. Rather,
    look for opportunities to express how you feel
    sorry when you see someone being on drugs, or
    expressing your concern for the parents whose
    children are on drugs, or showing some articles
    of accidents and deaths that involve drugs and
    alcohol in some tactful ways.

9. Avoid even playfully saying, "I love you.... will
    you do this for me?" It dilutes the message of love
    with conditional statements. Your child will feel
    manipulated.

10. Learn to speak in a new and positive way and break the old patterns. And when we fall back into old patterns of condemnation or negativism, we must be courageous enough to own our problems and apologize to our children. . . . Always be willing to apologize to your children.

The benefits of learning how to speak the words of affirmation are many: You are raising a child with high self-esteem, and your child will know how to speak the same love language in turn to you.

Children who have been parented to understand they have value will still falter and fail, but most of the time they will get back up to write their next chapter. When the page turns from childhood to adulthood, they will understand their value has nothing to do with performance, but is an intrinsic attribute of their sacredness and is unconditional.

Consider the tragic children of this world who have been forced to measure their worth by their performance. They have been emotionally abandoned. Seldom are they encouraged or praised, often due to the pathetic and misguided notion that too much praise dilutes the value of supposedly earned and deserving praise.

2—Your Children Learn Best in Relationships

One of the simplest ways to measure psychopathology is to look at the quality of relationships that someone enjoys. Healthy, happy people have strong and lasting relationships in their lives. This is not about being an introvert or extrovert, this is about the core longing in a human being to connect with another. Human beings are made for relationship; therefore a second value to consider for your family is that relationships are more important than accomplishments, results, or tasks. This value is especially difficult because relationships are often painful. Our tendency to be self-serving and short-sided often gets in the way of relationships. Within each relationship there will be conflict, disappointment, aloneness, and commonplaceness. A family value that teaches children to push through these inevitable difficulties will position them for a richer life full of friendships and meaning. All humans must live with the tension between vulnerability and safety. They will be more capable of navigating this tension if they possess the value that relationships are worth the cost.

Humans are relationship-driven creatures. We need each other, and will go to amazing, sometimes scary lengths to feel accepted by and connected to others. The fact that we are made for relationships is an important reason to teach your children manners. Manners seem like a lost art form these days, but manners are really just a matter of learning how to treat others well.

TEACHING MANNERS FOSTERS EMPATHY

Manners are a codified way each culture has for keeping things pleasant even when we'd rather not. The specifics may differ from country to country or region to region but the intent is much the same. Every language has words of courtesy. Every culture has generally understood rules for polite interaction. Training in those codes starts very, very young. As we teach our kids the words and rituals, the manners, of our culture, we are laying down the foundation for genuine empathy later on.[4]

---

4 Marie Hartwell-Walker, "Teaching Manners Breeds Empathy in Children," PsychCentral (2013) accessed November 16, 2015, http://psychcentral.com/lib/teaching-manners-breeds-empathy-in-children.

Do you want your child to stand out above the crowd? Teach them manners. Manners are rooted in kindness, in helping others feel at home; they are the grease that oils the machine of social interaction. And they are different in different cultures. The better your manners are, the more places you will feel at home; conversely, manners should never be used to put another person below you.

I see parents fretting over whether their child gets all A's in school, or how they score on the SAT college preparatory exams, or if their artwork gets selected to be displayed in the school hallway showcase. Intelligence is important. We want to train our children to think critically and to be smart, to "use their head for something besides a hat rack" (as my father would say). However, there will always be someone smarter than your child, someone who scores higher on a test, who can draw better, run faster, or sing better. But a very simple way for your child to stand out, be noticed, and distinguish themselves in this world is to teach them manners. Entering a room and confidently introducing oneself or waiting to begin eating until everyone has been served are simple ways to show respect and treat others with kindness.

When you hear a child consistently say "please" and "thank you" when speaking, or when he or she addresses an adult as "sir," or "ma'am," you notice, and you're impressed. Manners correctly illustrate respect for others simply because they are humans and have value. Modeling manners for your children demonstrates to them the value of others and reinforces this value that you have written on your storyboard. Be intentional in teaching your children basic manners. Our society has become incredibly hedonistic and me-centered. Raising children to care about the needs of others and to be selfless in a selfish society is no easy task. But I promise you that people who have a heart and concern for others are happier people in general.

All of us desire to be happy, to be comfortable. But life is uncertain and hard. Bad things happen to good people. Your comfort and happiness will be threatened. If you raise children to put themselves first, they will be inward- focused, selfish people. They will also be ultimately miserable. Everything that threatens their contentment and happiness will be seen as a threat, which will isolate them from interacting with others and being loving toward those around them. Instead, raise them with the understanding that life is not about being happy or being comfortable. It's about living with a sense of mission and purpose. It's about being someone who makes the world a better place by putting others first.

#3—We Can Make a Difference

The choices we make impact the world around us. From the moment we first begin movement and thought, neural pathways are created in our brains. They are the railway system that connects one part of our brain with another and each time the same pathway is used, it is deepened. A child who cries for milk will quickly learn to repeat that exact cry if they are fed each time. If a child feels acceptance each time your eyes meet, that child will seek your face. Even in infancy, that child's story begins to be written. What you choose to reinforce in your child matters, and with that choice comes great responsibility. Your child should learn that the community in which they live should benefit from their presence. If they experience grace and empathy and see you extend those attributes to others, they will follow you and enhance the world. Should children in third world countries receive the benefit of your child's generosity? If that is a value to you, speak about the struggles of others in the world and teach your child how they can impact the world for good.

As humans, we are also endowed with the ability to think and choose for ourselves whether that choice be for good or for evil. An important value that we want our children to embrace is the fact that they are not robots—they can think and choose for themselves. But with that amazing gift of choice comes an equally amazing

> *Human beings are made for relationship.*

reality; there are consequences to every choice we make. We want our children to know that they can make choices and that they need to consider the consequences of their actions before they speak or act. Unlike in video games and movies, life doesn't allow many "do-overs."

Call someone an idiot and it's out there. The damage has been done. All you can do then is salvage the relationship with a heartfelt apology. You ride your bike into the street without looking, and heaven help you if a car is coming and the person driving is not paying attention. An accident happens, and all we can do is deal with the trauma and damage that results. There's no rewind button on life. As soon as a child can understand the word "no," you can begin to teach consequences. If the child reaches to hit the cat's nose, talk through the scenario. Tell your child "no" and then explain the possible consequences of hitting a cat. Even though your child will not understand all of what you say, you have begun the process of teaching decision-making and natural consequences. This dialogue will soon become a habit and you will be modeling the process of choice and consequence.

It's fashionable in our culture to look for a scapegoat—someone else to blame for our decisions. But raising children to be responsible means raising them to accept the consequences for their decisions. Kids need to know that they are given an amazing responsibility: the power of choice. Foolish choices can bring destruction. Wisdom must accompany the power of choice.

Many children are afraid to make decisions. This is often because the child is not realistically measuring the importance of the decision. If they choose the blue truck instead of the red truck, does that mean that they will never receive another toy? Of course not, but they need to realize that even though they will certainly receive another toy, this will be the truck that they will be playing with for some time. Talk them through the decision-making process. When appropriate, let them listen as you and your spouse make thoughtful decisions. The ability to make decisions and live with the consequences is an important theme for your family story. Kids who can do this have a far greater likelihood of being influential and successful as adults than kids who are afraid to make a decision or are unwilling to own up to the consequences of the decisions they do make.

The ability to make decisions and live with the consequences is an important theme for your family story.

The facts that our children are sacred, that we are all created to be in relationship, and that we can all make a positive difference are only a few values that we consider important. There are many other values and character traits we could list (for instance, forgiveness, caring for the less fortunate, having dreams, taking risks, and being thankful). These are all wonderful values and character traits that we need to intentionally exhibit in the home. Remember what we learned from the previous section on "reflecting." Values are embraced when you consistently demonstrate them in the home. The values our children embrace are "caught not taught." Live these values and your life will be their classroom; try to teach them without living them, and your words will likely be ignored.

WHO'S TO BLAME?

Who is to blame for childhood obesity? According to a survey of parents by ACNielsen, there's plenty to be had:

- Only 1% of parents blamed manufactures
- 7% blamed advertising on TV, etc.
- 9% blamed the child
- 10% blamed fast food companies

And not surprisingly, two thirds of parents blamed themselves. After all, especially for younger kids, parents are the only ones that have control over all of these things. Parents can help their kids make healthy food choices, both at home and when eating fast food, can limit TV watching and time spent playing video games, and can encourage kids to be more active.

Of course it isn't easy, especially if the parents themselves are overweight, but teaching our children to make healthier choices is essential if we want them to be healthy and avoid the health consequences of being overweight.[5]

---

[5] Vincent Iannelli, "Childhood Obesity," About Heath, updated January 26, 2008, http://pediatrics.about.com/cs/nutrition/a/blame_obesity.htm.

Chapter 5

Building Freedom to Choose Well

"I THOUGHT I RAISED YOU BETTER THAN THAT!"

ALL CHARACTERS IN a story are initially presented as static. They become dynamic as they make choices during their interaction with the other characters, the setting, the plot and the direction of the story. Children are born without the ability to self-soothe or be effective decision makers. They are static or what some might call "foolish." We want our children to become dynamic or what some might call "wise." It is the goal of the parent to move their child toward maturity, independence, and responsibility. The journey between foolishness and wisdom is filled with peril. Along the way, we all make

decisions that cause the journey to become much more difficult. How can we teach our children to make good decisions?
We must provide the structure and the safety to allow them the
opportunity to fail.

There are a few basic principles on this path between foolishness and wisdom. To begin with, pick your battles. There are
many black and white issues where you can apply this formula:
good behavior + consistency = trust, and trust = freedom. Children
must learn that it is necessary for good health and hygiene to
brush their teeth. As infants, the job is ours. As they grow into
toddlerhood, we often allow them to hold the brush while we
complete the task. By kindergarten, they are brushing, but we
may supervise. Finally, when we see that they are consistently
brushing well, we may simply remind them of the task. In reality,
I have reminded my kids to brush even in their late teens, but the
responsibility belongs to them. They have

Pick your battles.

earned freedom from supervision by dis-
playing responsibility and wisdom. These
black and white decisions are often quite simple to make, but
there are many "grey areas" where the decisions are not matters of
right and wrong but are matters of taste and culture.

What color their bedroom is painted, how long they can
wear their hair, how short their skirts can be, how many pierc-
ings they can have, whether their bed needs to be made—these
are all areas that can be discussed and negotiated. As much as
we can be tempted to invoke moral absolutes, we need to be
able to discern the subjectivity of cultural morays (including
our own). Just because we can't stand a style doesn't mean that
it is intrinsically evil. My daughter was eighteen when she got
her first tattoo. She was legally an adult, I did not pay for it,

and it was actually a nice tattoo. Still, I am a member of a generation that generally relates tattooing with other vices. We talked about the wisdom she had shown in having the tattoo placed on her shoulder so she could choose when it would show. It was not a moral absolute that I could rant about, it was a matter of taste, and so I let it go. The storyboard, themes, and narrative direction that you have chosen for your family will help you decide which battles to fight.

The combination of a growing maturity and trust in your child will allow you to give them more freedom. But how does one measure maturity? We know that age is not the best predictor. You are the best judge of your child's maturity. Ask yourself, how consistently do they follow through with responsibilities? Are they able to control and divert their frustration when unforeseen events alter their plans? Many families believe that all children should be given the same freedoms when they reach a specific age. But all children are different. You must weigh the factors of safety, abilities, and previous choices when making these decisions, and your choices for your kids will not always be popular.

Lev Vygotsky, a cognitive theorist, explains the process of child development by using a scaffolding metaphor. When a child is learning or performing a task that they are not competent or confident with, an adult should assist. That adult acts as scaffolding by supporting the child as they grow in ability. As the child becomes more adept and stronger, the assistance must become less to allow the child to flourish. Eventually, the scaffolding or adult will be completely removed from the child.[6]

---

[6] http://study.com/academy/lesson/zone-of-proximal-development-and-scaffolding-in-the-classroom.htm

The teenage years can be especially challenging, in part because your kids are exposed to influences beyond you. The options and opportunities to make both right and wrong choices are magnified exponentially. Though our tendency as parents is to shield our children from making bad choices by making good choices for them, we need to instead coach them through the decision-making process.

Part of that "coaching" requires that we be willing to share openly about some of the poor choices we have made along the way, not just to be relatable but to help children avoid unnecessary and often harmful consequences. I have seen many nineteen-year-olds blow up when facing their first independent decisions at college. They were not properly prepared for all of the choices and not aware of all of the consequences that their solitary decisions could create. We all make mistakes. Parents who love and support their children through their mistakes and the consequences of those mistakes are not necessarily condoning or enabling bad behavior.

TOWARD ADOLESCENT INDEPENDENCE

How much independence should I give my child?

As children enter adolescence, they often beg for more freedom. Parents walk a tightrope between wanting their children to be confident and able to do things for themselves and knowing that the world can be a scary place with threats to their children's health and safety.

Some parents allow too much of the wrong kind of freedom or they offer freedom before the adolescent is ready to accept it. Other parents cling too tightly, denying young teens both the responsibilities they require to develop maturity and the opportunities they need to make choices and accept their consequences.

Research tells us that adolescents do best when they remain closely connected to their parents but at the same time are allowed to have their own points of view and even to disagree with their parents. Here are some tips to help balance closeness and independence:

- Set limits. Setting limits is most effective when it begins early. It is harder but not impossible, however, to establish limits during early adolescence.

- Be clear. Most young teens respond best to specific instructions, which are repeated regularly.

- Give reasonable choices. Choices make young teens more open to guidance. Using humor and creativity as you give choices may also make your child more willing to accept them.

- Grant independence in stages. The more mature and responsible a young teen's behavior is, the more privileges parents can grant.

- Health and safety come first. Your most important responsibility as a parent is to protect your child's health and safety. Your child needs to know that your love for her requires you to veto activities and choices that threaten either of these.

- Say no to choices that cut off future options. Some things aren't worth fighting about. It may offend you if your son wears a shirt to school that clashes wildly with his pants, but this isn't a choice that can cut off future possibilities for him. On the other hand, he may not skip school and he may not avoid taking tough courses that will prepare him for college.

- Guide, but resist the temptation to control. Strike a good balance between laying down the law and allowing too much freedom.

- Let kids make mistakes. We want our children to grow into adults who can solve problems and make good choices.

> - Make actions have consequences. If you tell your child that she must be home by 10 p.m., do not ignore her midnight arrival. You lose credibility with your child if she suffers no consequences for returning home two hours late.
>
> Finally and despite what we often hear and read, adolescents look to their parents first and foremost in shaping their lives. When it comes to morals and ethics, political beliefs and religion, teenagers almost always have more in common with their parents than their parents believe. As a parent, you should look beyond the surface, beyond the specific behaviors to who your child is becoming.[7]

With Freedom Comes . . . Responsibility

If you don't obey the laws of the road, you will likely find your license suspended. Similarly, if your teenager cannot adhere to the laws about underage drinking, they should face an appropriate consequence such as not being allowed to attend events where alcohol is being served. You want to give your child more and more freedom to make his or her own choices, but you also have a responsibility to ensure that, to the best of your knowledge, they will make a wise and healthy choice.

It's a very simple formula. Freedom requires maturity, and maturity is evidenced by good choices, and good choices build trust. Therefore, more trust means more freedom; less trust means less freedom.

---

[7] U.S. Department of Education, "Independence—Helping Your Child through Early Adolescence," accessed November 16, 2015, http://www.ed.gov/parents/academic/help/adolescence/part7.html.

CONSISTENCY—LOVE IN MOTION

For your words and your rules to be accepted by your maturing child, they must be evenly enforced and lived out by everyone in the family, including you. One of the most vivid examples of this in our home, and quite frankly an area where I struggle, is with driving. I'm an aggressive driver. I think I'm a good driver in the fact that I am aware of what's going on around me. But I've been known to drive faster than the speed limit and often make aggressive moves that can make my passengers feel uncomfortable...or so my wife tells me. So as each of my sons learn to drive, I realize that my advice and direction is negated, or at least marginalized every time they see me drive differently than I require them to drive. What are my options at this point? Either revert to the old "Do as I say, not as I do" philosophy (which we established in chapter 3 doesn't work all that well), or hope that my kids have enough sense to decide for themselves, "I want to be a better driver than Dad."

Neither is a good option. But as my story hopefully illustrates, no parent does everything perfectly or as he or she should. Hopefully the principles we are discussing here you can take to heart and apply in a growing number of areas in your life.

As your children get older, they are going to press the boundaries, challenge the rules, and wherever possible, push your buttons (especially by identifying your own inconsistencies). That's a normal part of the growing and maturing process. Your responsibility is to be consistent, to stay true to the storyboard, and reinforce the theme of the story that you are writing. You must reflect the beliefs, values, standards, priorities, and rules that you hold dear. You do this by first living them out in front

of your kids (your actions) and by consistently promoting and
enforcing these things through your words. And when you do
fail, you do what is best—you swallow your pride, apologize,
and stand by the truth of the values behind the rule.

In this section, we have realized that although we are the
most important influence in our child's life, it is good for our
child to have other role models. We should establish core values
for our family and live those values on a consistent basis. What
you believe determines your values, and these values form your
priorities. The most difficult aspect of this section to live out is
the slow release of total control of all of your child's choices to
allow them to learn the value of good choices.

PARENTS SET POOR EXAMPLE

You're in a rush, so you drive hurriedly. You've got oh-so-
many responsibilities, so you try to catch up via cell phone
during the commute. When you're pooped from trying to
keep up, you still get behind the wheel.

Sound familiar?

State Farm surveyed more than 1,000 parents or
guardians of teen drivers this summer and the picture
that emerges shows parents are operating in the "do as I
say, not as I do" world:

- 65% of parents admitted to talking on cell phones
  behind the wheel, even as more than
- 90% said they restrict their teen drivers from doing so.
- 68% of parents drive while they are in a hurry at least
  occasionally—prime circumstances for speeding and
  other unsafe behaviors.
- 65% fess up to driving while tired from time to time.

For some of us, that's life. But parents are passing on
habits that put us all at risk.

"Kids tend to model after their parents, whether we like it or not," said State Farm spokeswoman Angie Rinock. "They're doing what they're telling their kids not to do."

. . . Be honest, parents, but tell it like it is, no matter how confident you or your teen may be in his or her skills and judgment.[8]

---

[8] Matt Helms, "Parent's Distracted Driving Habits Set a Poor Example," *Free Press Columnist*, October 20, 2008, http://www.freep.com/article/20081020/COL12/810200325.

Directing—The Plot of Your Family Story

Chapter 6

Knowing Your Child

"YOU DON'T KNOW HOW LUCKY YOU
ARE. WHY WHEN I WAS YOUR AGE..."

A GOOD MOVIE DIRECTOR notices special chemistry between certain actors and quickly makes adjustments to the script to explore the possibilities. This concept translates easily into the family relationships. For instance, does your eight-year-old have better nurturing instincts for your pet than her twelve-year-old brother? Why not expand on that inclination by offering books, trips to the zoo, or educational material for her? Be a curious parent, always looking for passion, rather than an angry or frustrated parent, trying make your child into something they aren't meant to be. Most of us embrace the places where we felt affirmed and alive (where we experienced praise, excitement, and positive recognition). Understandably, we avoid those places where we feel death (humiliation, embarrassment, and pain).

How We React in Crisis

Our family moved from Tennessee to Orlando, and it was a difficult move. One of our children had a particularly stressful time adjusting. She became much more orderly with all of the objects in her room, which is not a bad thing, but she also became very anxious. When one feels as if they have no control over their situation, they sometimes become extremely controlling over anything in their power. One evening I went into her room to talk about my observations. I intentionally moved one of Rachel's mementos as I sat down. She became very agitated and nervous. As we talked through the situation, she began to realize that it wasn't really disorganization in her room that was causing her stress, but the move and her loss of what was known to her. One of the factors that added to her discomfort was her innate temperament.

Temperament is a particular style of relating. It is not something that your child has chosen. They were born with a specific, innate hard-wired method with which they experience and interact with the world. The ability to understand your own temperament and to be able to read the social cues that reveal the temperament of others is one of the basic components of social intelligence. It is also a great skill to model to your children. A good story director doesn't try to change their child's temperament, but rather helps them discover how to enhance the strengths of that temperament while minimizing the weaknesses.

The ability to understand our child's temperament will help us to better understand their potential. Everything in creation has a purpose. Hammers are made to drive nails, cars are made to drive people, and teenagers are clearly made to drive their parents crazy (just kidding...). People are created with design, intent, and purpose just like tools and trucks. But for many parents, this is a completely novel concept. How many times have you heard a well-intentioned parent say to his or her child, "You can be anything you want to be"? It's just not true. If you've ever seen me play basketball, you know that no matter how much I might want to play in the NBA and believe that I can, it simply isn't going to happen. I don't have the temperament, talent, or physical ability to cut it. But even if I did, is playing in the NBA what I was meant to do? More and more researchers, psychologists, counselors, and motivational speakers are writing books and giving seminars about how each of us has a "sweet spot" we can operate in, where we experience ultimate purpose, meaning, significance, fulfillment, and joy in life.

What these experts are tapping into is simply the concept that each of us has a unique set of talents, skills, and abilities. We are more likely to find fulfillment when we operate in the areas of our "gifting." To put a more spiritual spin on the concept, each of us was created by God with a unique "divine destiny" or plan, and when we calibrate our lives to that plan, viola! We create a much more compelling story and are able to live in it with more content, comfort, and success.

Parents should not raise their children to be whatever they want, but rather to be what they were created, destined, and gifted to be. Keep in mind that even if you understand your child's temperament and do all that you can to assist them in thriving, they still have the ability to make bad choices. If you are the parent of an adult child, realize that even if you did everything as perfectly as is humanly possible, you can only offer opportunities and guidance. Are they important and impactful? Yes! But are the effects a scientific absolute? No. Parents influence the outcome, they do not determine it.

Some suggest that one's identity is determined by what they choose to do in crises. James Marcia, an influential theorist who expanded upon Erikson's theory of identity crisis and identity confusion states:

> "Certain situations and events (called 'crises') serve as catalysts prompting movement along this continuum and through the various identity statuses. These crises create internal conflict and emotional upheaval, thereby causing adolescents to examine and question their values, beliefs, and goals. As they explore new possibilities, they may form new beliefs, adopt different values, and make different choices." According to Marcia's theory, these developmental crises ultimately cause adolescents to develop a progressively greater commitment to a particular individual identity via the process of identity exploration prompted by developmental crises.[9]

That is an academic way of saying that we simply need to be aware of the crises in our kids' lives and help direct them to make good decisions during those times.

Our commitments help us discover and shape our identity. Crisis is relative. When a fourth-grade girl forgets her locker

---

[9] Angela Oswalt, "James Marcia and Self-Identity," MentalHelp.net, November 17, 2010, https://www.mentalhelp.net/articles/james-marcia-and-self-identity.

combination, it feels like a crisis. Depending upon how she has learned to deal with her emotions and how well she has matured, it may still be a crisis at age seventeen. Helping your child learn how to respond well to a crisis (or what they perceive as a crisis at the time) is one of the best ways to direct your child toward a bigger story. It is in these moments of transition that a child develops a style of relating and begins understanding the circumstances of the world around them. It is important for parents to move beyond just giving the right answer, they should

> *Parents should not raise their children to be whatever they want, but rather to be what they were created, destined, and gifted to be.*

use these opportunities to understand their child, to listen, to empathize, and yes, also instruct. Help your child think of alternatives the next time they feel angry or embarrassed.

Who You Are is More than Just How You Behave

Identity is not just your personality, but how a person views, values, and understands themselves. My youngest son Jason went through a season in his life where the story he told himself was that he was the black sheep of the family, that he wasn't as smart or as "good" as his older brothers. It didn't seem to matter how often we told him how great he was or how proud of him we were. The voice in his head that he was choosing to listen to was louder than mine. So Jason started making choices that matched his identity. His grades suffered. He started hanging out with people who weren't challenging him to be better, but rather were enticing him to party more, to underachieve and settle for a small story. It was a tough season for him and for his mother and me. Through it all, we continued to believe (and pray) for the best for Jason and at every opportunity we reminded him of his value, his destiny—the bigger story for which he was made to live. We encouraged him to not let his behavior set the bar for his value and worth. Most of us have kids who go through these seasons. The season may be short or long, but can be frustrating and frightening. However, I want to encourage you not to give up. Words matter, and while my son spent several years settling for a smaller story, ultimately the better voices began to prevail.

As a parent, pay attention to how your son or daughter defines themselves. Do they define themselves by their strengths and potential, or by their failures and shortcomings? We all have both. But a key challenge for you in shaping your family story is to help each character in your script see themselves in the most positive light as possible and define their value and worth by who they can be, not just by what they

Parents influence the outcome, they do not determine it.

have done. For example, if Hannah diligently sets aside time to study her Spanish, completes all of the homework, and is still unable to make an "A" in class, how should you react? You can either chide her about her lack of ability or you can point out her excellent work ethic and diligence. You can tell Hannah how her dedication and ability to follow through are tremendous assets to assist her in her goal of becoming the best physical trainer in the area.

Our children's identity and sense of self will determine much of how they interact with their world. Identity is like very wet cement that becomes firmer over time.

I was sitting with someone in my counseling office the other day who could barely look at me due to the shame that he felt.

He expressed that regardless of what he attempts, it is inevitable that he will fail. He could try to be a little better, maybe choose to change a few things, but he would ultimately lose, because he sees himself as a loser. I find that someone with a shame-based identity often has a more difficult time when someone treats them with dignity rather than disgust. As we delved into the choices and events, decisions and

> *Our children's identity and sense of self will determine much of how they interact with their world.*

traumas that shaped this identity, some hope emerged. He realized that it might be possible to see himself differently.

Identity Impacts Behavior

A parent can help shape identity by putting words and choices to difficult situations. Remember, children do not develop abstract reasoning until they are adolescents. Therefore, they have a hard time connecting their heart and head. They have difficulty understanding cause and effect. Developmental Psychologist, Eric Erickson, suggested that at every epoch of life there is a task that a child must accomplish.

It would be helpful for the parent to be aware of the transitions that a child will go through and the approximate age. The major task of adolescence is identity development. Adolescents look for validation and vision. Validation tells them that they have what it takes and vision says there is a journey worth taking. Validation says that you have the tools. Parents need to discover where they are getting their validation and how they perceive the future.

Søren Kierkegaard said, "Surely this generation will die for its lack of passion." Passion is a strong commitment, enthusiasm, and compelling emotion toward a cause, activity, or even person. Sadly, it is often used today to speak only of sexuality. The word is derived from the Latin word for "suffer." It implies that you are so committed to something, someone, or some purpose that you would willingly suffer to protect or maintain it. Passion is that intangible feeling that makes humans feel alive. So often, when we teach a career class at the school where I work, people will ask the question, "What does the world need?" Not a bad question, but a more primal question may be "what makes you come alive?" The world around you needs to interact with people who are truly alive.

It is important, as parents, to develop a curiosity about not only your child's temperament, but also their passions. I have a passion for entrepreneurial ideas and my wife has heard me start a hundred businesses at our dinner table. In spite of my lack of musical ability, my son comes alive when he plays music. Our daughter seems to be in a different world when she works with young children. We can never be free of our deepest passions, we can only bury them. Eric Little, the subject of the movie "Chariots of Fire," once stated, "I feel God's pleasure when I run." Over the years, talent shows have become very big on TV—American Idol, The Voice, American's Got Talent, So You Think You Can Dance, etc. Typically the first few episodes show both the worst and best auditions. When I watched an embarrassingly poor audition that succeeded only in humiliating the person, I wondered, *Where are their parents? Why didn't someone shape, encourage, or redirect their passion before they became the joke of a nation?*

Passions are often very fragile during the tender years of a child's life. Praise and encouragement and curiosity play an important role in nurturing the natural passions that your child may possess. Even if you are not interested in drama you need to be willing to allow your child to explore his or her interest and nurture that interest if it's there. If your grandmother loved playing the piano and you are not very interested in it, it would be still good to expose your child to the instrument. Consider the physical characteristics that your child possesses. As a toddler, does he possess great hand-eye coordination but is only in the 20% for growth? He may be great at gymnastics, rock climbing, music, etc. Does your daughter constantly redecorate her room or her doll's house? She might have an innate knack for art and creativity.

Passion is a wonderful thing. The good news is that it cannot only be cultivated, it can be redirected. If your child's skills and temperament do not agree with their passions, your job may be to redirect. Your 5'1" son may never be an NBA player, but his knowledge, passion, and commitment to the game could combine to make him a great coach. I am by nature a very creative person. Now I barely know how to turn on a computer, much less be fluent in today's complex design software. Yet, through much of my career I have interacted with designers, writers, and musicians, and have had opportunity to participate in the creative process.

The adolescent experience is a dress rehearsal for life, and the parent's job is to provide direction and feedback.

The adolescent experience is a dress rehearsal for life, and the parent's job is to provide direction and feedback. My middle son Darren has a passion to help the weak, to defend the poor, and to stand up for those who cannot stand up for themselves. Darren is very strong and athletic. He's competitive and likes to win. But I've come to understand that one of the reasons Darren is strong is so that he can literally run with the weak. Darren has a heart of compassion, and as Darren began competing in school sports in middle and high school, I noticed that if he was asked to be a team captain, Darren would often pick a less talented person to be on his team. Why? His competitive nature would suggest that he choose the most talented kids to be on his team. But he instinctively had a heart of compassion for those who are weak or less fortunate. This is something that, as a parent, I need to encourage, not discourage. In seasons in life when I have seen Darren perhaps stray from this built-in passion and direction, my job as a parent is to remind him of who he is, and call him back towards the way he was created to go.

What careers will your kids have? Who knows? But remember this: what they do for a living is not the only way to measure the way they are called to go.

My oldest son is a communicator. I can't fully explain why, but I have a sense that this is part of the purpose and path for David's life. So as his parent, I want to help him develop his communication skills. Will he wind up being a broadcaster, a politician, or an advertising executive? I don't know. But as he grows I can help him hone his communication skills. With most strengths come corresponding weakness. So when I see my son becoming hot-tempered, letting his emotions get the better of him, or when he uses his communications skills to berate or belittle, I need to call him out on that.

Your awareness of the specific purposes and calling for each of your children will unfold over time. If you're like me, you won't wake up one morning and have everything figured out.

It's a process. Your child and their abilities, personality, and desires will become more apparent throughout childhood and adolescence. Observing your child throughout the various situations of life and being attune to the way that they respond will enhance your ability to assist their growth. Discovering your child's passion and direction requires you to pay attention. Watch to see what causes your child's eyes to light up.

Once you have discovered some of these passions, be willing to walk outside of your own comfort zone to allow them to explore. You are the guide, the one who must make the difficult call if the interest is too dangerous, not age appropriate, or financially impossible. If at all possible, make adjustments so that your child can develop a healthy passion. Try and understand what it is they enjoy the most about it. You must provide direction and correction. Undisciplined passion will lead more to addiction than to success.

Never use your child to fill some aching need for affection that you have.

There are many parents I have counseled who failed to provide needed direction and correction because they are afraid of wounding, discouraging, or frustrating their kids. Sometimes they are just plain afraid of their kids. Parenting is not an easy job. Any gratification that you receive could be years—maybe decades—in the future. You will make mistakes. You will wound and frustrate your kids at times. But continue to move forward. Apologize to them, and let those situations become valuable life lessons.

Do not fail to live up to your responsibilities because you are afraid that your son or daughter will not like you. Never use your child to fill some aching need for affection that you have.

One of your jobs as a parent is to give affection. This is your unconditional responsibility whether or not that person gives it back to you, or seems to deserve it.. If you discover that you are shirking your role as a parent in order to meet some of your own needs, by all means, for the benefit of your family story, find ways to work on those issues.

Your job is to raise your child right, to train him or her in the way to go, regardless of whether that makes you likable or popular. Maybe you were the picked-on kid in school growing up and now find yourself being the popular "cool" parent. That's great. But don't confuse being a "popular parent" with being a great story director. Kids need you to be their parent, not their buddy.

> *Kids need you to be their parent, not their buddy.*

Behind most people who live with passion is someone who helped direct them toward that passion.

To live in the sweet spot of life, a parent must direct their child to understand the big story of the world and how their natural skills, temperament, and passions play into their role in the big story of life.

Chapter 7

Helping Your Child Find Their Way

"WHO IS THIS KID? I DON'T UNDERSTAND WHAT THEY'RE THINKING!"

PARENTING PHILOSOPHIES ABOUND, but most theories fall within two main camps. Much of parenting literature will advise you to allow your child to discover who they are and what they are to become. Purists in this camp believe that if you shape and direct in any way, you are dictating the child's life and eliminating their natural inclinations. Children should be allowed to self-determine all aspects of their lives including their values.

The other extreme is the parent who lives vicariously through the child and forces them to participate in specific activities that the parent believes the child may excel in, whether or not the child is interested. Neither extreme is likely to produce the kind of story you want for your family. You would never drop a young child in an uncharted forest without maps, directions, advice, provisions, and directions. And yet you would want them to experience the wonder of the forest and take in the adventure—even face danger. But your ultimate goal is that they find their way through the forest successfully as well as enjoying the journey. Your responsibility is to ensure safe passage while highlighting both the beauty and danger along the way. No one appreciates a guide who simply tells you where the destination is located. It is the guide's responsibility to make sure that the young explorer can understand and appreciate what they are experiencing while doing your best to ensure they stay close enough to the path to successfully navigate the perils and pleasures of the forest.

There is a biblical proverb that says if you train a child in "the way he should go," then when he is older, he will not depart from it (Proverbs 22:6). There is a "way" your child is designed to go. The way they should go is a reference to the way that a reed bends in the wind.

A good parent will become curious about their child's temperament and personality. There are countless personality tests— some compare your personality with the traits of a particular animal, some will give you letters, some descriptive words. All of the tests attempt to categorize people into broad categories in which they typically interact with others. Many disagreements that we have with others during our lifetime are not issues of right and wrong, rather they are differences of temperament and perspective. For example, an extrovert may marry an introvert. Extroverts often process out loud as they think and garner energy from interaction. Introverts must think about things before they say them, and they re-energize from being alone. Once the couple understands the way that their partner experiences life, an understanding balance can more easily be achieved.

We must treat our children with the same curiosity and respect. Extroverts typically begin the morning engaging others in conversation, whereas an introvert may need a little quiet time to begin the day. Neither of these morning rituals is right or wrong—they are simply different. The grid or temperament with which you experience life will dictate much of your default parenting. I am an extrovert, and before I realized that my youngest son was an introvert, I expected him to be able to blurt out information when asked a question. If there was a problem, I expected him to be able to recount the people, circumstances, and situation along with his emotions almost immediately. It took some time before I realized that in order to properly retell his experience he needed to be given some time to effectively process his experience.

A good story director knows the temperament of the characters in the story. You might be an extrovert who tends to process out loud. You can easily share what you're thinking (whether anyone is asking or not). However, your spouse or your child may be an introvert, someone who thinks deeply but will need more time to internally process and express their thoughts. Don't expect them to interact and process the way that you do.

The Way

Going back to Proverbs 22:6 (NKJV), "Train up a child in the way he should go and when he is old he will not depart from it." Notice the proverb does not say train up children to be successful. It does not say train them up to be good. It says train them up *in the way they should go.* Isn't it a relief to know that there is a unique plan, a chosen way for your child's life? There is a way in which he or she should go.

Your responsibility is to help your children make true and right choices, to help them discern the way that is best for

> *Your responsibility is to help your children make true and right choices, to help them discern the way that is best for them.*

them. So much of what we hear in popular culture is that parents should take a "hands off" approach and let each child discover for themselves what is the way, the path of life that's right for them. But to shape a great family story requires just the opposite. Don't sit back and trust fate or destiny to guide your child's life path. Be attentive to sense the direction, the path, the way they are uniquely designed to go, and lovingly and intentionally—even relentlessly—direct them in that way. That's how you shape a great family story.

It is often difficult for trained psychologists to determine the relational styles of very young children, but you can learn a great deal about the way that your child experiences life by observation. Is it very important for them to have yes or no answers, or do they seem comfortable with "maybe"? Are they slow to warm up to a group of people but comfortable with one person at a time? Do they like to be the center of attention or are they more content to watch and consider what is going on around them? Again, there is no right or wrong answer. These are simply clues to the way that your child experiences the world, and therefore helpful hints for the best ways to communicate with that child. Like good movie directors know the characters in their films, parents should know their children well enough to be able to emphasize strengths, minimize weaknesses, and correct when needed. Your child's temperament will help you discern some measure of the way in which he or she should go. Going back to our forest ranger analogy, a truly gifted guide will discern what things to point out, what things to pursue, and what to avoid along the journey in the forest that will match the child's innate, God-given temperaments and inclinations. The director is not a dictator. There is a difference between guiding and demanding. As a parent, sometimes you have to be firm and simply say, "stop doing that," especially with younger children. But as they get older, sometimes it's more effective to hold up the mirror and help your child see how their behavior is affecting the storyline of those around them.

We challenge you not to take the passive approach to parenting by leaving all decisions up to the child. Help them discover the wonderful story they were created to make. Help them capture every ounce of majesty, wonder, and adventure in their journey through the forest of life.

Chapter 8

Living in a Big Story

"WHY CAN'T MY CHILD BE MORE LIKE _____?"

W ITH DOZENS OF TV's buzzing, and loud conversations about football, it is amazing that any real conversations take place at Buffalo Wild Wings. But it has become a favorite place for my son and me to meet and chat. A few years ago, we had one of our "wings and words" meetings concerning his plans for the future. My son is an amazing musician, and as he finished high school he and a garage band of friends began enjoying increased popularity performing at local venues. He decided to postpone his college education, dreaming instead of making it big in a music genre with a limited following. As a man who has lived his life in the world of academia, I had always assumed that my son would immediately pursue higher education. Instead, he decided to take a summer job as a white water river guide at a camp in the Carolinas. As I wished him well for the summer, I gave him some advice that selfishly was difficult for me to offer but I knew in my heart it was the right thing to say. "If you find a good group of kids who are going to a good college, consider not coming back home. It's okay if you stay." I then added, "It's not that I don't want you home I will miss you terribly. It's just killing me to watch you live in such a small story."

Everyone begins life in a small story. Developmental psychologists tell us that initially an infant understands the world only from the perspective of what they can see and touch. Without direction we will still childishly believe that we are the center of a small story. The call to a bigger story echoes in life. We hear it in the laughter of our grandparents and the vastness of the sunset. It calls us in the paradox we experience as we look at the ocean... the simultaneous feeling of significance and insignificance. There is a calling in

> *Everyone begins life in a small story.*

humanity that reminds us that there is a larger story. Children will not find their role in this story on their own. You are the director. You must teach your child to leave the small, egocentric story of oneness so they can embrace and fully understand that they are living a much bigger story. You can impart the vision that their life is part of a much greater plan.

The idea of living in the big story entails fighting three common lies. The first lie in living a small story is that the world revolves around you. We are born selfish; an infant can sense only its own needs. This is a purposeful trait in the way we are designed. This self-centeredness allows our children to let us know when they are hungry, ill, or simply need to be held. Without this "selfishness" our children would not survive. As we faithfully meet those needs, we can begin to model the ideals of empathy, altruism, sharing, and kindness. No longer solely "self-focused," a child can begin to express an outward "others-focus." This taps into the noble, even divine aspects of our human nature. As a parent, you have a critical role in helping your child mature from a small, self-centered view of the world to the bigger story. Your toddler will watch the way that you interact with your dog, slam your phone in anger, or roll your eyes at your spouse's comment. You should begin to talk about your actions and reasons: "I pet Nikko because dogs need affection." When your child sees an action that you do not want him to model, explain the reason why it is inappropriate: "I should not have slammed the phone. That was rude of me, wasn't it?" Give words to actions, and speak motives and results aloud. In a celebrity-driven culture, the myth that the world revolves around you is a significant myth to debunk. As a psychologist, I have never seen someone who focuses entirely on himself who is emotionally healthy.

The second lie of living a small story is that I can live life without others. This goes beyond what was stated in the previous chapter. We have already established that what we do affects others and that we are designed to be in relationship with others. The reality is that if you are to live in the big picture, you must realize that you are part of the community. Christian tradition says that every follower of Jesus is considered a member of one universal body. The imagery is powerful. The actions of one person are exponentially more effective when working as a member of a cohesive unit with others. To be optimally effective, we must be a part of the community. The examples are numerous: a great violinist is a treasure to behold, but when he is a member of a symphony, masterpieces are performed and a fullness of the musical spectrum is achieved that is impossible with only a singular instrument. Allow your child to participate in a group that has a specific goal, like choir or soccer. Help them to understand the power that is present when many work for a common goal.

The third small story lie is that one person cannot change things. It is better to have one person committed to a cause than ten people who only express half-hearted interest in it.

It is counterintuitive to a child to believe that their story will make a difference. You can demonstrate this principal by conscientiously pointing out to your child the difference that their actions make in your home. Make certain to point out the positive impact that your child is contributing to the family: "Thank you for helping to clean the kitchen, now we have time to play a game." "Teaching your younger brother to throw the ball well has really helped build his confidence. You really made a difference." Praising your child by pointing out how their actions have affected those around them will encourage your kids to see that they make a difference. Also state when the contrary occurs: "You played too long and did not finish your homework, therefore none of us can go to Baskin Robbins for ice cream tonight."

I have never seen someone who focuses entirely on himself who is emotionally healthy.

Model these principles in your home. If you want your kids to be concerned about the needs of the poor, to have a kind and caring soul, then let them see those values in you. Do you want them to work hard, be diligent, and always willing to go the extra mile—to do more than what's expected of them? Then let them see you live it. Living a big story is not the same as living an extravagant life. Sometimes the biggest stories occur in the most humble of settings. A courageous single mother who parents her child wisely while being the sole income and director for her home may not feel as if she is impacting the world, but her choices will.

Section Four

Protecting—Creating a Positive Setting

Chapter 9

Protection from External Influences

"KIDS ARE GROWING UP SO FAST THESE DAYS. I DIDN'T HAVE TO DEAL WITH THESE ISSUES UNTIL I WAS IN MY 20'S"

GOOD STORIES OCCUR in all sorts of "settings." They can be realistic like a good police drama or fantasy filled such as a CIA operative assigned to be a family babysitter. Some settings are fairytale and fanciful while others are horrific and toxic. We can't raise our kids in a cultural bubble. But as a parent we can be diligent to provide safeguards and boundaries that will help our child live well even when the setting of their life is not what we envisioned. What do you do when the values that are popular or accepted in the culture don't line up neatly with your own?

My wife and I believe that sex is an amazing, wonderful component of the human experience. We also believe that what Hollywood feeds us through television and movies reduces sexual intimacy to simply a biological function that is about as common as blowing your nose or eating a bowl of cereal. We want to create a setting for our children that places a high value on sexual intimacy. Clearly we are swimming against the tide. We have to be intentional in training our children with this value because it is not reflected in our contemporary culture. As parents, we have to be careful to guard our children's hearts and minds from harmful influences every bit as much as we need to put up appropriate safeguards to protect them physically. My wife told me that I had exposed our son, Jason, to too much sexuality at too early an age through what we watched on television at night. I had to agree with her. While I have never brought pornography into the house or explicit movies, the fact that I allowed him to watch some PG-13 movies and even R-rated movies—and some television shows—with crude sexual humor and innuendos means that I was creating a setting for him that was inconsistent with our sexual values. I was more careful about these things with Jason's older brothers. But as often happens with parents with multiple kids, it's easy to relax and become a little less strict in raising the children who come later in the birth order.

It is natural to let up, but you must provide a safe setting for your child's story that matches your values and beliefs. If you have toddlers, you would naturally secure your kitchen cabinets, ensuring that toxic cleaners are out of reach of curious arms and fingers. Even if you are a stay-at-home mom or dad, you can't watch your child every moment. It only takes a few

seconds for a curious two-year-old to swallow something poi-
sonous. When kids are older, the clear and present dangers in
your home might not be the drain cleaner, but perhaps alcohol,
prescription drugs, or a gun. Paying attention to where and
how you store things is just part of what it means to have a safe
home environment. It's your job as the parent to make your
home physically safe for your kids, and safety measures change
as they get older.

Continual discussions with your children will assist you as
you decide how quickly or slowly you release the controls in
your home. Our daughter loved all types of sweets as a child
and would constantly try to search them out, while our son
never developed a taste for sugar. Even though we would have
let him have a treat on the rare occasion that he desired one, we
had to keep them out of reach to help our daughter control her
impulses. As she matured and was able to alter her behaviors,
we altered ours. Now, all things are accessible to her because
she successfully developed some self-control.

There is a difference between protection and isolation. We do
not suggest you should sequester your children and make them
live in a bubble from the '50's. Don't let your parenting become
fear-based. Give your kids a healthy appreciation that they are
part of a global society made up of a diverse mix of values and
interests and they need to get along with others who are different from them. Fear is a good short-term motivator, but it
does not sustain for the long term. Instead, let your motivation to protect come from a desire to see your kids become all
they can be and were created to be. I protect my children from
things that could numb, discourage, or exploit them. It is also
my desire and responsibility to protect their ability to dream, to

learn, to risk, and to cultivate faith, hope, and love. I want their potential to be limited only by their choices and God's direction, not by the damage inflicted by others or by our culture. Let's examine some of the external things (outside of the family) that might affect the setting of our children's story.

Protecting From Things That Numb

Life is a constant battle between living in reality—which is full of tension, pain, and pleasure—and living in a fantasy world. Fantasy can initially feel comforting, but robs us of truly living. Every child must learn healthy self-soothing strategies in life. An infant cannot self-soothe, and is dependent upon others. A sign of maturity is being able to deal with disappointment and discomfort in healthy ways. An unhealthy tendency is to find things that make us numb. For young children, it might be the constant droning of the TV for hours upon hours. Even programming designed for children will allow them to disengage their minds and place them on "cruise control." Teens might find their comfort in video games, music, or social networking. Often the things that numb us are good in small doses, but numbing when taken to an extreme. Numbing has an effect that is opposite to what one might expect. Exposing children to inappropriate horror or violent movies can desensitize them to the feelings of others and lessen the realization that there are natural consequences for behavior. These are not necessarily R-rated movies. Be wary of movies that glorify or "smile" at violence or the mistreatment of others. Video games that place women in a demeaning light have the potential of destroying the possibility of true sexual freedom. Consistent exposure to a particular stimulus is always desensitizing, although it does not always produce a change in behavior. One child may be exposed to pornography and never seek it out again, while another may immediately become obsessed with the material. The images that are seen through the eyes of children or hormone-raging teens cannot be unseen. Teens can become numb through sports, academics, food, or almost anything that consumes one's time.

At some level, the seeds of addiction live in a commitment to numb. There is a fine line between protecting your children from other people and circumstances and allowing them to taste and learn to deal with disappointments and discouragements. For young children, fantasy and imagination, imaginary friends and places are fine. In fact, it is extremely important for young children to be encouraged to dream and imagine. Just remember that it is difficult for young children to know what is truth and what

> *Don't let your parenting become fear-based.*

is fiction. That is why age-appropriate filtering of media is important. Hollywood does not care if your kids grow up confident, healthy, and secure; their interest in your child is simply monetary. Therefore it would be wise to place boundaries on your children's access to media.

Sarah is the child of a friend who was adopted at the age of nine. Before her adoption, Sarah had lived in a variety of situations, and many times she was without responsible adult supervision. When she was almost fifteen, she told me that she had always wondered what it would really feel like to slice someone's arm with a knife. When I asked her why she was curious, she explained that she had watched her first Freddy Kruger movie at the age of four. During her first nine years of life, her mother loved slasher/horror movies and did not consider the impact on her child. Some children might have become very frightful and paranoid, but it made Sarah curious. She spent time considering what it would feel like to commit a crime against another person, something that she should have never had to witness on screen.

Protect From Things That Discourage

Not only do you protect your child from things that numb their senses and their hearts, but you need to protect them from sources of discouragement. Your children should be challenged with realistic and reachable goals. While an unrealistically high goal will discourage, a goal that the child can easily attain will make the child comfortable with mediocrity.

Discouragement and disappointment have a way of sticking with a child, so children should be challenged but not pushed to the point of discouragement when they study, compete in athletics, or complete their chores. I don't know if I would have become a good architect or not, but I vividly remember when I let go of the dream. I was in the ninth grade and, due to scheduling constraints, I was placed in a third level drafting course as an elective. The class standard was so far above my ability and the teacher so negative towards my initial feeble attempts, that the budding designer in me threw away his drafting pencils, never to pick them up again. To this day, my wife, who has a beautiful singing voice, gets very uncomfortable singing in public. Why? Because in her freshman year of high school she was asked to sing a solo alto part in her choral class that she wasn't prepared for and ended up being laughed at.

Isn't it amazing how loudly those silent voices in our heads can scream at us? Watch out for coaches, church leaders, and teachers who motivate by shame or humiliation. There is nothing wrong with a dance teacher, pastor, or coach expecting accountability. But shame, humiliation, and guilt have a way of discouraging children. It is imperative that the "self-talk" a child begins to repeat in his or her mind is positive—"I can do this when I really try," "I am a kind person"—rather than self-loathing and derogatory statements. Well-intended people can begin a destructive process by giving their child internal messages such as, "I will never be able to do that," or "I am not smart enough," etc. And if you have multiple children, pay extra attention to not comparing one child to their siblings. Our

Isn't it amazing how loudly those silent voices in our heads can scream at us?

youngest son for years told himself he was the "black sheep" of the family, not as smart as his older brothers. His life took a dramatic turn (for the better) when he started playing a different tape in his head.

Protect From Things That Exploit

Although we have stated earlier that we must protect our children from becoming numb, there are times when it can occur and the parent not even realize there is a problem. If, for instance, your child is a diligent student and spends many hours in their bedroom, there is the possibility that more than studying for school is occurring. In case a numbing or desensitization has occurred, you must also protect them from those who might exploit this opportunity. I stated earlier that Hollywood does not care about your children, and neither does McDonalds.

They both see children as a place of revenue. They don't necessarily want to harm your children. There are, however, those who do. The vast majority of people on the internet are just like you and me, but there are those whose intent is evil. Your child must be protected from physical, sexual, and psychological abuse. Nearly 70% of all reported sexual assaults (including assaults on adults) occur to children ages seventeen and under.[10]

Protecting your children will not always make you popular with your children, especially if you have teenagers. But it is your responsibility as a parent. Monitoring on-line activities is no longer an option in today's world. There are many different programs that you can purchase to block inappropriate sites but there are also highly rated free programs such as K9 Web Protection, Windows Family Safety and Avira Free Anti-Virus. If you choose to allow your children access to the internet, computers, cell phones, and media, it is your right to monitor and establish guidelines for that access.

HOME CONDUITS OF DESTRUCTION

In the past, pornography was mainly limited to artwork, magazines, and the red-light districts. With the advent of the Internet and cable television, however, pornography has now made its way into our family rooms, home offices, and kids' bedrooms. It is easily—and often inadvertently—accessible by children and teenagers, and parents must work even harder to prevent their children from becoming addicted to it (Larry Eldridge, Jr., CWK Network, Inc.).

[10] Howard N. Snyder, "Sexual Assault of Young Children as Reported to Law Enforcement: Victim, Incident, and Offender Characteristics," US Dept. of Justice, Bureau of Justice Statistics, National Center for Juvenile Justice, (July 2000), NCJ 182990.

If children constantly feed their minds with pornography (and I'm not just talking about hardcore porn, but "soft porn" like you see in magazines and catalogs of the swimsuit-edition and lingerie varieties), they may find it very difficult to understand how to have a healthy and loving sexual relationship with their spouse. Sex therapists argue that a child who watches pornography at an early age will likely have a harder time finding sexual fulfillment and satisfaction in a "normal" (non-airbrushed, real-life) intimate relationship.

Whether you live in a mansion in the Hollywood Hills or a row house on the south side of Chicago, the place you call home needs to be a place of safety. By *safe* we mean that no matter what I do or how I perform, I will always be loved and cared for. Safe means that your child can admit (confess) anything and know they will always be valued and heard. Safe means that the home will be free from influences such as violence, pornography, drugs, and other things harmful to a child.

Often, negative influences stem from a good and natural desire that is taken off track. We are all created with a positive and healthy desire for adventure and beauty. Where the story gets corrupted is when those natural and positive desires are derailed and we settle for something far less ideal that brings a short-term satisfaction tied to long-term pain.

The damage that is done to your child's heart, spirit, and mind through the natural process of life can be minimized if your home is strong, safe, and secure. Home is the place where you must make your stand and expend the most time and energy to make it secure.

Pornography's Impact on Marriage and the Family

The research indicates pornography consumption is associated with the following six trends, among others:

1. Increased marital distress, and risk of separation and divorce
2. Decreased marital intimacy and sexual satisfaction
3. Infidelity
4. Increased appetite for more graphic types of pornography and sexual activity associated with abusive, illegal or unsafe practices
5. Devaluation of monogamy, marriage and child-rearing
6. An increasing number of people struggling with compulsive and addictive sexual behavior.

These trends reflect a cluster of symptoms that undermine the foundation upon which successful marriages and families are established.

While the marital bond may be the most vulnerable relationship to Internet pornography, children and adolescents are the most vulnerable audience. When a child lives in a home where an adult is consuming pornography, he or she encounters the following four risks:

1. Decreased parental time and attention
2. Increased risk of encountering pornographic material
3. Increased risk of parental separation and divorce and
4. Increased risk of parental job loss and financial strain

When a child or adolescent is directly exposed the following effects have been documented:

1. Lasting negative or traumatic emotional responses
2. Earlier onset of first sexual intercourse, thereby increasing the risk of STD's over the lifespan

3. The belief that superior sexual satisfaction is attainable without having affection for one's partner, thereby reinforcing the commoditization of sex and the objectification of humans.

4. The belief that being married or having a family are unattractive prospects

5. Increased risk for developing sexual compulsions and addictive behavior

6. Increased risk of exposure to incorrect information about human sexuality long before a minor is able to contextualize this information in ways an adult brain could.

7. And, overestimating the prevalence of less common practices (e.g., group sex, bestiality, or sadomasochistic activity).[11]

---

[11] Jill Manning, "Pornography's Impact on Marriage & the Family," The Heritage Foundation, November 9, 2005, http://www.heritage.org/Research/Testimony/Pornographys-Impact-on-Marriage-amp-The-Family.

Chapter 10

Protection from
Internal Influences

"BUT I NEEDED A FRIEND TO TALK TO
ABOUT MY TERRIBLE MARRIAGE, AND
MY DAUGHTER WAS HAPPY TO LISTEN."

H E HAD BECOME an angry and fearful man. Andy was attempting to salvage his broken marriage. As he recounted his family and his childhood, he remembered how dedicated his parents had been to him, even if they weren't to each other. They homeschooled him to protect him from questionable influences. They controlled his television and media exposure. They provided him with significant religious instruction. Yet, he did not know how to have healthy relationships and was struggling with the ability to understand or control his emotions and actions. He says he always knew that his parents disliked one another, and that he had become his mother's confidant. He had become the rescuer of the family, preventing it from imploding.

She was a cheerleader but it seemed to be more important to her mother than to her. When she was voted "most popular" or class president, the entire family cheered, but if she failed, the entire family was depressed, even angry with her. Her successes seemed to be the only thing that her family valued, and if there was a failure, it was monumental for her mother. She realized at the age of twelve that the weight of her mother's self-esteem was riding on her—and that weight was heavy.

It is our responsibility as parents to guard our kids from harm. This means we must have a game plan and be willing to set clear boundaries for what our children can do, what they can view, who they can hang out with, and where they can go. It is always easier to talk about the external things from which we must protect our kids. However, the most significant damage can often come from internal sources inside of our home, not external sources. As you strive to shape your family story into something your children will want to fondly retell to their kids someday, put your emphasis on paying attention to the relational dynamics that happen behind closed doors when only your child is listening. Invest in building a memorable plot that will be a remarkable story for generations to come.

The Balance Between Connecting and Individualization

We all know a family that seems too close. At first and from a distance it looks enviable. However, as one moves closer, the family begins to feel sticky and smothering. Family systems research and literature will often call this enmeshment.[12] You want your family to be a team in which all players have roles and responsibilities and can work together toward a common goal, yet, it is imperative that the individual children also be allowed separate identities.

Connectedness, family cohesiveness, and secure attachments must be balanced with autonomy and separate identity as is appropriate for each developmental age. Once your child becomes an adult, they must be able to switch their predominant loyalty to their own spouse and family without guilt.

The other extreme is a family that is disengaged. Family members may feel simply like roommates, or more seriously, like prisoners who are captive in a secure but sterile environment. Parents must monitor the tension between enmeshment and individualization. It is important to note that these two values will be fluid and change as the child develops over time. Young children will need more of your focus to be on attachment and trust-building whereas teens need more independence and responsibility.

There are two parenting movements that overemphasize opposing sides of the continuum. The attachment parenting movement makes attachment the primary goal of early interaction—don't misunderstand—attachment is crucial for healthy child development. This approach, however, is so extreme that it can make it difficult for a child to learn how to self-soothe. All needs are so quickly met that discomfort is not allowed. The child can become extremely dependent. The other extreme program promotes scheduling all of the care functions of your infant, including sleeping, eating, and playing, and adhering

---

[12] 2013, Randi Kreger, *Psychology Today*, *Stop Walking on Eggshells*.

strictly to the schedule regardless of your infant's needs and cries. Many pediatricians rightly advise that this extreme method of child-rearing can increase the possibility of malnutrition, failure to thrive, and emotional disorders.

Parentification

A damaging problem that has lifelong effects is the parentification of a child. As illustrated with this chapter's opening story, parentification can occur when a child has become his parent's confidant. It is fine to talk to your children about increasingly complex topics, but parent-child differentiation can begin to break down when the child feels the weight of an adult decision is upon them. This process may coincide with the beginning of the breakdown of the parent's marriage, and it may very well escalate the process. Initially, if one parent is seeking a confidant and the other spouse is uncomfortable with such closeness, placing the child in the position of an emotional (not sexual) surrogate can ease tension. But as the child develops an innate push for development beyond the family, this growth will destabilize the fragile marriage relationship. Both parents will be angry because their demands and needs are not being met and the child is placed in the impossible position of holding a family together. I know this is a tough subject, especially in a culture where the majority of parents have experienced divorce and separation. It is incredibly important to our children's emotional well-being to know that they can count on Mom and Dad always being there for them—that the most sacred and significant environment they know, their home, is something they can count on.

The home environment should be nurturing and promote trust, security, love, and the ability to dream and risk. That environment can quickly become toxic when Mom and Dad allow their relationship to deteriorate.

Fighting Parents Impair Kid's Emotional Development

"Everyone will have fights now and again that are pretty negative. Children are not fragile this way. It is only when there is an accumulation of negative fights that the children lose confidence in the emotional security of the family." University of Notre Dame psychologist E. Mark Cummings, PhD, and colleagues. . . .

The fights that hurt kids—and parents—may have some or all of these negative features:

- Defensiveness
- Personal insults
- Verbal hostility
- Nonverbal expressions of hostility
- Stonewalling
- Physical aggression. All experts tell WebMD that physical violence is enormously damaging to children's emotional well-being.

The fights that don't hurt kids—and which may actually help them—have many of these constructive features:

- Problem-solving
- Compromise
- Expressing positive feelings in the context of conflict
- Making supportive statements
- Verbal expressions of affection

(Quoted from article by Daniel J. DeNoon, "Fighting Parents Impair Kid's Emotional Development," Feb. 09, 2006, FoxNews.com, WebMD.)

Suppose you find yourself in a one-parent environment due to divorce, or you are in a troubled marriage. Please don't feel guilty about your situation. Seek the help and assistance that you need to make the best of this difficult circumstance. Don't try to talk yourself into thinking that caustic, hurtful, and dysfunctional relationships in your family don't seriously impact your children. First, make the commitment to work through your issues with your spouse or partner. Communicate honestly and listen—really hear your partner's perspective.

> Children in homes of divorce must be protected from feeling as if they are being used as a weapon in the adult battle that is occurring, or has occurred in the family.

And as you work through your relationships, please apply this simple principle: "Take it outside." In short, work through your issues someplace other than in front of your kids—especially if you can't seem to do so in a gracious, kind, and thoughtful way. You are the parent. You will always be the parent. They are your children. Remember, if you are already divorced, children in homes of divorce must be protected from feeling as if they are being used as a weapon in the adult battle that is occurring, or has occurred in the family.

Rigid Roles

Another destructive type of dysfunction within a family is caused by rigid roles among the members. In a dysfunctional family one child often takes the role of a rescuer, one parent is the persecutor, and the other is a victim. These roles can become solidified, such an automatic behavioral default, that the child will play that role in every relationship. Empathy is important, but is it really best for your child to seek friendships only from people they believe that they can rescue from a bad situation? If you allow your child to continually play the victim, they will seek out others who always play the rescuer. Obviously, this is not the basis for a healthy peer relationship. The role of the persecutor will also establish a lifelong personality trait if not dealt with quickly. If your child learns that they can have what they want by pushing, yelling, or even hitting someone, that method will become their default process of success. The persecutor often becomes the bully in life.

Teaching Kids Not To Bully

It can be shocking and upsetting to learn that your child has gotten in trouble for picking on others or been labeled a bully.

As difficult as it may be to process this news, it's important to deal with it right away. Whether the bullying is physical or verbal, if it's not stopped it can lead to more aggressive antisocial behavior and interfere with your child's success in school and ability to form and sustain friendships. . . .

Let your child know that bullying is unacceptable and that there will be serious consequences at home, school, and in the community if it continues.

Try to understand the reasons behind your child's behavior. In some cases, kids bully because they have trouble managing strong emotions like anger, frustration, or insecurity. In other cases, kids haven't learned cooperative ways to work out conflicts and understand differences. Be sure to:

1. Take bullying seriously. Make sure your kids understand that you will not tolerate bullying at home or anywhere else. Establish rules about bullying and stick to them. If you punish your child by taking away privileges, be sure it's meaningful.

2. Teach kids to treat others with respect and kindness. Teach your child that it is wrong to ridicule differences (i.e., race, religion, appearance, special needs, gender, economic status) and try to instill a sense of empathy for those who are different.

3. Learn about your child's social life. Look for insight into the factors that may be influencing your child's behavior in the school environment (or wherever the bullying is occurring). Talk with parents of your child's friends and peers, teachers, guidance counselors, and the school principal.

4. Encourage good behavior. Positive reinforcement can be more powerful than negative discipline. Catch your kids being good—and when they handle situations in ways that are constructive or positive, take notice and praise them for it.

5. Set a good example. Think carefully about how you talk around your kids and how you handle conflict and problems. If you behave aggressively—toward or in front of your kids—chances are they'll follow your example. Instead, point out positives in others, rather than negatives.[13]

(Quoted from "Kids Health," The Nemours Foundation; http://kidshealth.org/PageManager.jsp?dn=KidsHealth&lic=1&ps=107&cat_id=146&article_set=58079).

Healthy parenting allows children to dress rehearse different roles, ideas, skills, and strengths which enable them to play the roles that are needed to be a healthy adult. There will be times in life where we must lead, follow, support, and defend, and our home must be a safe venue to practice all of the skills.

---

[13] D'Arcy Lyness, reviewer, "Teaching Kids Not To Bully," KidsHealth, July 2013, http://kidshealth.org/PageManager.jsp?dn=KidsHealth&lic=1&ps=107&cat_id=146&article_set=58079.

Abuse and Betrayal

A myriad of books and journals are dedicated to the extreme damage that abuse and betrayal within one's family can do to a child. A child inherently realizes that parents, grandparents, relatives, siblings, and caretakers should protect them. When one of these people who are within the "inner circle" of a child's heart betrays that trust, the possibility for a lifetime of bad choices and emotional illness is raised significantly. This is especially true for very young children who have not yet developed the ability to think abstractly and the damage from abuse may take a lifetime to repair. Take notice of any changes in sleeping, eating, and mood behaviors in your children and ask if anything is troubling them. Obviously, a solid trusting relationship that has been previously established with your child will allow truth to flow much faster. If the child mentions any type of abuse, act immediately to protect, treat the child, and prosecute if applicable. The response of a parent in believing and actively pursuing openness and resolution about the event will go a long way in beginning the healing process.

Despite their protests, children instinctively understand that love is often expressed in what we say they *can't* do even more than what we say they *can* do. If you sense any type of hesitancy from your child when a neighbor or even a relative asks to spend time alone with the child, investigate the situation. It is better to overreact than underreact in these situations.

PROTECTING FROM MEDIOCRITY

Adapting the Rules As Your Child Matures

We have mentioned that it is detrimental for children to have rigid roles that they feel they must play to keep the family functional. It is also damaging to maintain rigid rules and controls that do not fluctuate based upon the maturity of the child. As children grow and develop they will naturally want to begin making their own choices. Many parents don't always navigate these transitions well. For instance, caring parents shouldn't allow their preschool children to play in the front yard by themselves without supervision. At the same time, a thirteen-year-old should be allowed to ride their bike in the neighborhood well out of the sightline of mom or dad (providing that you live in a fairly safe neighborhood). By age eighteen your child may be driving a car across town. With each stage, the risk of harm to your child increases. And the choices they have to make are increasingly broad with more significant consequences if the wrong choice is made. So what do you do? How do you allow your child to stumble and fall, yet make sure there is a reasonable safety net there for the times when he or she messes up? These are tough questions with which every parent must grapple.

> All kids need to experience failure . . . and all of them will.

It is often with fear and trepidation that we must make the decision to give our children greater freedoms. But it is important to allow them to experience successes and failures within the relative safety of our homes. Some sixteen-year-olds are mature enough to drive to the mall, choose an acceptable movie, and return home with no problems while others are simply not ready. These decisions will be more difficult if there is an issue with joint custody of a child, but consistency, if at all possible, is important.

Learning How to Let Go

How can leaving your home and learning to let your child be independent protect them from an in-home threat? While an essential aspect of being a parent is providing appropriate safeguards, so too is learning to let go. Part of how we grow and mature as individuals is through failure. All kids need to experience failure . . . and all of them will. You don't learn how to ride a two-wheeler without a few tumbles, scrapes, and cuts. Few of us find our way into a loving marriage without having our hearts broken sometime along the journey.

Life is not a sure thing—it involves risk. As a parent, you need to eliminate the unhealthy risk while at the same time encouraging your son or daughter to take reasonable risks and be comfortable living with uncertainty and risk. If you bail them out of every dilemma or every uncomfortable situation they encounter, you are impeding their ability to leave your home. They will have neither the confidence nor the tools to deal with difficult situations on their own. We can initially teach children to risk a little pain by playing rock-paper-scissors, where the measured consequence may be getting a hand slapped by the opponent. That is very different from giving an untrained teen the keys to your car and letting her explore the world alone.

My son was on a snow skiing trip with some college friends. We got a call from him from the hospital. Apparently he had snowboarded off the slope and into a tree . . . the tree won. He had no major damage, but apparently was knocked out and had to be brought down in a stretcher. That night on the phone, as he related the story (and was more embarrassed than wounded), my reaction was totally different from that of my wife.

I said, "So how soon can you get back out on the slopes?"

My wife gave me her typical look that only she can do...the one that says, "Are you mental?"

You see, once I knew David was okay, I wanted to make sure that his encounter with a tree didn't cause him to shirk back from continuing to work on his snowboarding skills. I wanted him to get back on the proverbial horse—or in this case, snowboard.

We all fail. We all get tossed off horses and hit trees. Becoming resilient happens best when as parents we learn how to let go. Part of living a great story is learning how to let go and teach our kids not to be quitters—training them to be comfortable with failure and risk. It may be safer to keep training wheels on the bike, but the sooner they learn to ride the bike without them, the happier they will be. By allowing your children to risk, you are teaching them to try things that are beyond their abilities, to stretch, to grow. You are expanding their ability to dream and believe what it is possible for them to do.

> *By allowing your children to risk, you are teaching them to try things that are beyond their abilities, to stretch, to grow.*

We all want to avoid pain, failure, and risk. And yet the experiences of pain, failure, and risk are key ingredients that make us healthy, happy, and successful people. As your children grow, let them know you believe in them. Encourage them to take risks and try new things. And when they fail (not if, when), you will be there for them. Then they will learn an even more important lesson: your love for them remains unchanged regardless of whether they win or lose, succeed or fail.

Chapter 11

Protection from
Eternal Dangers

"SOMETIMES I WONDERED WHAT THEY WERE LEARNING IN SCHOOL, BUT I FELT TOO INTIMIDATED TO ASK HIS TEACHER."

S HE IS SO mean!" This was Skylar's most common comment about one of his teachers when he was in school. Learning facts and figures has always been almost impossible for him. Anyone who tried to teach him was often the object of his anger.

One facet of Skylar's autism is his tendency to place thoughts into a "revolving door" from which it is difficult to escape. His first year of school in a new city was fodder for continuous outbursts, and his new teacher was the subject of many of them.

Moves are stressful for kids like Skye, and we convinced ourselves that his complaints about this teacher were just part of his readjustment. We should have listened to him more closely and observed his teacher more carefully when we visited the school. She was eventually arrested for abusing some of the students with autism in the room. Although Skye was never the physical victim, he witnessed her actions. My son became a witness against her. It has been several years since his experience with this particular teacher, but if someone corrects him abruptly, he will say, "You are just like Mrs. Smith." If an event totally unrelated to that experience upsets him, such as a fire alarm or strong storm, he will grab from his stash of Nerf guns and begin walking the inside perimeter of our home to protect us. Before too long, the initial fear of the storm will morph into a fear that "she" is outside.

This teacher forever colored how my son sees authority. He believes that someone is after him; he often distrusts what those in authority say to him. I know that year was exceptional and so is he, but that year he became the protector of all the other kids against the mean teacher. He learned that authority is not to be trusted. It has so affected his life that he has trouble working and dealing with other teachers. He does not trust authority, and sometimes he even questions ours.

I share this personal story to illustrate a powerful truth: What we believe will determine many things about how we live. After twenty-five years in the counselor's chair I have identified some very important beliefs to address. As you attempt to protect your kids from external threats and internal threats— also be aware of these "eternal threats"—beliefs that can either harm or enhance their life.

How You Perceive Authority

We all must live under some level of authority. We will have teachers, bosses, parents, police, and the government. How a person perceives and responds to authority will determine much about their quality of life. Over the past thirty years I have taught thousands of students. Each one is in my class to learn the specifics about a subject that I am teaching. It is interesting to view their response to my words from my perch in front of the class. It takes very little time to determine which students have a problem with authority. There are some who want to question each statement and seem to feel that challenging others is their duty. Everyone is a potential threat and their mission is to attack all of those with power. You are your children's chief authority figure. Therefore you are in the best position to teach your children about honoring and respecting authority. Children should be taught respect but must also be aware that power should always be accompanied by accountability.

As a child grows, one of the most important skills for them to develop is the ability to read and understand authority. If you always question everyone in a position of power, regardless of status and situation, life will be much more difficult. Many who struggle with chronic unemployment have difficulty following instructions and listening to authority. Those who cannot learn from the knowledge, wisdom, and advice of those who are farther along in the journey are destined to live a life of conflict and make avoidable mistakes. However, to blindly follow everyone who has power can have significant and sometimes dire consequences as well. Reasonable authority will allow conversation and accountability.

I am reminded of the time that my daughter returned home from one of her college classes. She was proud of the way that she had corrected her teacher in front of the class. She recounted the interaction sentence by sentence. It was not over a moral issue; it was over the correct interpretation of a piece of literature. It was also the only class that she had to repeat in college. It would have been appropriate to ask questions and express her point of view, and we have taught her to do so. But somewhere in that classroom, a battle was won and the war was lost. The teacher perceived her as disrespectful and unteachable and her grade reflected that opinion.

Parents have the opportunity to model fair, respectful, and honorable authority. The respect of authority has implications that echo into eternity. How one views authority will have significant effects on their perception and understanding of God, and their view of the universe.

Authority is experienced differently depending upon where you live. In some countries and communities there is much talk and energy devoted to limiting government. In other places, people realize that their government is protecting the citizens from exploitation, and the call is often heard for increased involvement. Understanding how to live with authority is not simple, but it is crucial.

Delaying Gratification

If you ask a five-year-old if they would rather have a Snickers candy bar now or a Maserati sports car when they turn eighteen, most five-year-olds would enjoy the Snickers now. That is because the concept of waiting a long time for a reward for work done today is a very difficult concept to grasp. This is yet another way that we are different from animals. Animals receive their rewards immediately; you cannot explain to a dog that they will receive a treat in an hour. However, we are more than Pavlovian animals. We can learn to delay gratification, but it is a trait that must be learned.

I am not sure that the spoils of life always go to the powerful, or the greedy, but they almost always go to the patient person with foresight and self-discipline. The ability to delay gratification and to do what is correct, right, or noble right now, even if the immediate value is not evident, is of eternal benefit.

How can you both model and teach this to your children as they write their stories?

Money and food may be the two easiest learning tools for delayed gratification. However, be aware that the external landscape of our culture does not reinforce the significant importance of this eternal principle. America is consumed by debt and owned by the holders of our debt, because we want everything now. It we don't have the cash, we use plastic. Many of our political problems are simply the result of politicians who do not have the courage to fix something long term when they must pay the short-term consequences (non-reelection) for it. A common expression in politics is to "kick the can down the road" and hope that the next group will remedy the problem. People who learn to delay gratification, to work toward a long term goal even if there is short term cost, will enjoy a more satisfying future. This can be taught by having a savings jar with change in it. Let your kids see that when the jar is filled, the family will enjoy a night at the movies. Our culture does not reinforce this belief, so it is important to show your children that money should be saved for a goal. This is also true with food and exercise. (My hypocrite meter is currently redlining.) Rewards follow the persistent work of those who can wait to enjoy the fruits of their labor.

Positive Work Ethic

I must admit that I like bumper stickers. It seems foolish to ruin a $30,000 car with a $2 decal, but I enjoy reading the philosophies that others feel strongly enough about that they will display it to the world at sixty miles per hour. Sometimes I wonder what people are thinking as I read their proclamations. There is one that comes to mind that proclaims, "I owe, I owe, so off to work I go," and another which states, "A bad day at the beach is better than a good day at work." Those may be true statements for the driver of the car, but quite frankly, I sometimes wonder where they park their cars at work. If I were their employer, I wonder if those would be the first people that I would lay off. These stickers may simply be signs of immature discretion, but they don't give the impression that the driver takes pride in his job. We have taught our children to always work as if they hold the position that is superior to them. If they can take that to heart, they will be looked at as first choice for that position. Similarly, an owner who has mortgaged her home to begin the business of her dreams will not tolerate seeing her nest egg thrown away on sloppy employees.

We must teach our children to be good stewards with their jobs, otherwise, they may not have one. I don't want my children to live to work, but I do want them to develop a positive work ethic that includes diligence and going the extra mile. Social media has blurred the lines between our professional positions and personal ones. I'm sure you've seen news stories about employees who admitted being rude to a customer on Facebook only to find out that what they thought they were sharing in a non-work-related venue quickly became evidence that resulted in their termination.

I meet with new employees at companies where I have worked and go over what I call the "Top Ten Character Traits of Success." At the top of my list is the character trait of "Diligence." To me diligence is simply having a can-do, go-the-extra-mile attitude. I have found that the employees that most often get ahead and advance in a company are the ones who simply have a great work ethic. They work harder than the average employee.

Resilience in the Face of Inconvenience

Life is hard—or at the very least, uncertain and inconvenient. It is full of disappointing moments and annoying setbacks. Developing resilience is an important skill. You want to raise kids who have the ability to bounce back, to get back on the proverbial horse when they get knocked off. Dr. Larry Crabb, a well-known psychologist, author, and Bible teacher says, "There is a little bit of something wrong with everything on this side of heaven." Another more "earthly" way of stating the same sentiment is summed up by the bumper sticker that says, "S#@% happens." Some temperaments and genetic predispositions may make it more difficult to be resilient; however the research would suggest that this is a critical trait that can be taught and developed.[14] Being able to put life events in perspective is an important aspect of dealing with the inconveniences of life. This skill is not natural to children and must be developed by parents.

---

[14] Martin E.P. Seligman, "Building Resilience," *Harvard Business Review*, April 2011 , https://hbr.org/2011/04/building-resilience.

I remember how my son felt when his first girlfriend broke up with him—I was struggling to figure out how to redeem his fourteen-year-old masculinity in the face of his first broken heart. I am not sure my actions were correct but my goal was to give and gain perspective, and to create something oddly positive in the midst of this event. We went to his favorite restaurant, and on the way back home I stopped and purchased two small, sweet cigars. After returning home we went out in the back to spend some time talking about life, love, and first kisses. I am not a smoker and am not encouraging you to buy your children tobacco, but I had considered the possibilities and had decided that this was a type of "rite of passage." I asked him questions about the relationship, specifically what he had learned about himself, about women, and about the woman he would want to marry someday.

The ritual became a tradition. At the end of each of his relationships, we eat at the same restaurant, buy the same cheap cigars, and have the same conversation. I think he may only remember the cigars and the good food. I was trying to help him gain perspective, to understand the positive life lessons that could be learned from the experience. As some of you read this, you may be focusing on the fact that I bought cigars for my son. What kind of parent, let alone a parent who is focused on directing a great family story, would do something like that? Let me reiterate, the point was not buying cigars. The goal was talking my son through a disappointing and inconvenient event with a new perspective. I was trying to teach him resilience, which, according to the Merriam-Webster Dictionary means, "tending to recover from or adjust easily to misfortune or change."

A GUIDE TO PROMOTING RESILIENCE IN CHILDREN: STRENGTHENING THE HUMAN SPIRIT

Edith H. Grotberg, Ph.D.
The International Resilience Project

How parents and other caregivers respond to situations, and how they help a child to respond, separates those adults who promote resilience in their children from those who destroy resilience or send confusing messages that both promote and inhibit resilience.

Three sources of resilience

To overcome adversities, children draw from three sources of resilience features labeled: I HAVE, I AM, I CAN. What they draw from each of the three sources may be described as follows:

I HAVE

- People around me I trust and who love me, no matter what
- People who set limits for me so I know when to stop before there is danger or trouble
- People who show me how to do things right by the way they do things
- People who want me to learn to do things on my own
- People who help me when I am sick, in danger or need to learn

I AM

- A person people can like and love
- Glad to do nice things for others and show my concern
- Respectful of myself and others
- Willing to be responsible for what I do
- Sure things will be all right

I CAN

- Talk to others about things that frighten me or bother me

- Find ways to solve problems that I face
- Control myself when I feel like doing something not right or dangerous
- Figure out when it is a good time to talk to someone or to take action
- Find someone to help me when I need it

A resilient child does not need all of these features to be resilient, but one is not enough.

For more information go to: http://www.bibalex.org/ SEARCH4Dev/files/283337/115519.PDF

Resilience is a fascinating phenomenon—a young boy's parents divorce, and it affects him the rest of his life. His next-door neighbor experiences the same heartache, and it seems to cause little change. One child deals with prejudice and poverty and uses the pain as a motivator to success and fulfillment, while another child in the same circumstance continues the cycle of generational poverty. From my years of listening to vulnerable people tell difficult stories, I have ascertained that the degree of support that the child experienced during a traumatic event is extremely important. This support does not always have to originate in the child's home. If a grandparent or parent listened to the child's fears, hopes, and dreams and then provided some type of grid for the child to gain a better perspective, they no longer felt as much fear. The absence of fear helped the child to garner the courage to once again begin to trust and take risks. The ability to risk and understand reasonable consequences, rather than imagined horrific scenarios, is resilience.

Other philosophical traits which will enhance your child's life would include developing a sense of humor, living with humility, and understanding the sacredness of human life. But for now the parenting discussion has begun about the eternal and philosophical areas in which we live.

So the question is, how do we get there from here?

Correcting—Conflict in Your Family Story

Chapter 12

Firm Limits, Gentle Grace

"WHY DOES IT ALWAYS HAVE TO BE A FIGHT?"

I HATE CONFLICT!" THAT'S what this woman said at the beginning of our first marriage counseling session. Most people don't care for conflict. And yet this woman's desire to avoid it at all costs contributed to a 20-year marriage that was now teetering on the brink of failure. This well-meaning couple had navigated around conflict for so long that when a significant crisis arose, they now found themselves helpless to know how to deal with it.

To create a great story, the characters must experience some form of conflict. In life we face conflict. It's unavoidable. The goal is not to live life devoid of conflict, but to help our kids learn how to handle conflict in a healthy way. Research suggests that one of the most powerful predictors of divorce or success in marriage is how a couple deals with conflict.[15] The style of conflict resolution that married couples use is often translated into their parenting style. The issue of "discipline" or "correcting" is a significant aspect of any family story.

My friend Stacia corrects a child by not just saying "no" but rather saying, "No, we're not doing it that way; but let's try this way." This kind of level-headed, unemotional parenting response comes more easily to some than to others. Some of us are hotheads. We are more volatile in all of our responses, whether it's someone giving us the finger in traffic or our four-year-old bringing his bowl of Captain Crunch into the living room and promptly spilling it on the carpet.

Regardless of your temperament, you can learn to respond better to your children when they make mistakes, push your buttons, or simply do something that irritates you. But before we get into some specific suggestions for ways to offer effective discipline and correction to your children, let's cover some core principles.

It is important to understand the four major styles of parenting. Typically, you will tend to default to one of these categories. Like it or not, you will probably parent like your parents. Maybe that's a good thing. But if not, you can change this pattern. We are often not good at judging our own parenting style; we generally tend to believe that our own style is the "right" style.

Diana Baumrind has done extensive research on the long term effects of different styles of parenting and discipline, and

---

[15] Gottman Marriage Institute

much of this section is derived from it.[16] Many researchers define the variables in this equation as Parental Control and Parental Affection—some may call it Restriction and Love. We will address the variables as limits and grace.

All parents have some type of limits on their children's behavior. We may be extremely permissive or excessively rigid, but the degree of control that you exercise over your child is your limit. We are also comfortable expressing differing degrees of affection. Some parents are very demonstrative and overt with praise and affection. Other parents may be more restrained, distant, or even uncomfortable with expressing affection. Affection in this scenario is not simply hugs and kisses. It is the manner with which you speak to your child. We will refer to this behavior as grace.

Authoritarian

The first category is known as the authoritarian style of parenting. It is characterized by parents who demand a great deal of control but demonstrate very little affection. Children are often instructed to obey their parents without any explanations or discussion. This can actually hamper your child's ability to develop reasoning and language skills. Consequences are not idle threats, and the children know this. These children learn to reign in their emotions, and are often perceived as being cold and distant. This is often referred to as "military style" parenting because the parents are interested only in being obeyed, regardless of the questions and concerns of the child. An

---

[16] Diana Baumrind, "The Influence of Parenting Style on Adolescent Competence and Substance Use," *Journal of Early Adolescence*, February 1991, 11:56-95.

example from TV would be Red Foreman, the father on "That '70's Show."

Children who have been parented in the authoritarian style are often successful in their chosen careers, but the discipline that they demonstrate has come at great personal cost. They have a hard time being vulnerable in relationships and have difficulty developing friendships. As adults they often suffer from low self-esteem and anxiety.

Disengaged

The disengaged style of parenting is characterized by demanding little of your children, and simultaneously giving them little grace or affection. They are most often ignored or pushed away. These parents may be wrapped up in their own dramas of drug abuse, alcoholism, mental disorders, or depression. The result, however, is that their child begins to feel invisible. They may consistently see themselves as unworthy of attention or act out so that they cannot be ignored. These children often become at-risk youth who have never developed a sense of identity. They often repeat this cycle of disengaged parenting with their own children unless they can break free with the help of counselors and others who will persistently pursue relationships with them.

In the event that other members of the home supply emotional and physical interaction and affection, the negative effects may be lessened. The mother of my friend, Sarah, was afflicted with what we now know was an untreated bipolar disorder during her childhood. Her mother, now nearing the end of life, has told Sarah that the only time she held her was during feeding. Sarah can remember going for weeks without hearing her mother speak, and she did not know why. Fortunately for my friend, she had older and younger siblings along with a "permissive" father who supplied her with affection and interaction.

Permissive

The permissive style of parenting has been prevalent in the baby boomer generation. Permissive parents provide few limits and restrictions along with much affection. These parents like the idea of being friends with their children. Their children are given too much control in the home, and outsiders might define them as "spoiled." Permissive parents are indulgent and often lack consistency. Their children often become demanding and dependent. As one might expect, permissive parenting is often practiced by those who grew up with authoritarian parents. They don't really believe they have the right to be the one in charge and make their children behave.

Heather was a very bright, attractive cheerleader in her small town high school. She was the only child of a business owner and stay-at-home mother who tried for years to conceive a child. She was voted "Best Dressed" each year, and received a new Mustang upon her high school graduation. Sarah had everything that any child could want, but her parents did not understand that what she truly wanted and needed were boundaries. Without any curfews and with the great powers of manipulation that she had developed, she was available for almost any activity or adventure. By the age of twenty-five, she had been married, divorced, and was a parent. She had never learned the discipline required to attend college. Depression led her to abuse prescription drugs to cope with her demons. Now, at the age of fifty-eight, she has been unemployed for twenty years, is addicted to alcohol, and lives off of her inheritance. There is no doubt that her parents loved her and that she made poor choices. But the lack of structure and expectations from her parents had a negative influence in the way her story has been lived.

Authoritative

Structure, expectations, firm limits, and bountiful warmth and affection constitute authoritative style of parenting. Do not be confused by the similarity of the names "authoritative" and "authoritarian." Although they may sound similar, they are very different styles. The authoritative style is the most balanced and effective of the four basic parenting styles. Rules are often explained and as the children become older, they are encouraged to discuss and help negotiate and set healthy rules and boundaries. Children are given clear, precise rules and guidelines that are consistently upheld by their parents. Discussions are encouraged, fostering communicative and reasoning abilities in the child. Parental warmth and affection are overt and frequently displayed. The children feel safe, knowing they are protected and secure in their home.

> *Discipline is a wonderful and essential tool that you must use lovingly, carefully, but consistently to ensure that your son or daughter becomes everything he or she is meant to be.*

Although the most effective parenting strategy, only 10-12% of parents actually provide authoritative Parenting. It is very common for parents to disagree about parenting styles, and even if both parents are in sync, many times there are other factors that influence parenting. The personality, birth order, and intelligence of the child can also influence the eventual style that the parents adopt. If the family includes a child with special needs, this can also sway parenting styles. The best family narratives are told by families who possess this balanced, healthy style of parenting. Good examples of authoritative parenting can be seen on the old reruns of "Little House on the Prairie" and the Camden's on "7th Heaven."

DISCIPLINE

In the authoritative style of parenting, discipline is not a punishment but rather a tool we use to shape character and to instruct our kids in how to behave. Discipline is essential for bringing all of us into our God-given potential. Discipline isn't about controlling children or controlling their behavior. It's not about making sure they feel the consequences of bad behavior. It's also not about venting your anger or frustration. Discipline is a wonderful and essential tool that you must use lovingly, carefully, and consistently to ensure that your son or daughter becomes everything he or she is meant to be. Discipline is a powerful act of love.

So how do you effectively discipline your child? We'll talk about this more specifically in chapter 15, but in general you need to keep in mind these three fundamental principles:

1. Clearly Communicate

You have to clearly communicate what is acceptable behavior and what is not. If you don't teach your child what is right and wrong, then disciplining for doing the wrong thing will come across to him or her as unfair and subjective. Kids need to know the rules before you start correcting them for breaking them.

2. Be Flexible and Variable

Second, you need to have more than one form of discipline in your child-rearing tool bag. If you only have one method of correction, you're in trouble. And the forms of discipline you use obviously need to change over time. Consider verbal correction, time out, taking away the use of toys, and writing notes of apology as methods of correction. No form of discipline should be done out of anger or frustration. The goal of your discipline is not punishment so much as instruction. Natural consequences are the most effective form of punishment. They mimic real life more than anything else. There are many more effective discipline techniques, and you need to be aware of them, try them, and figure out which ones are most effective.

3. The Consequence Fits the Crime

Third, you have to make sure the crime fits the time. Applying too much discipline for a small offense and too little discipline for a significant offense will limit the effectiveness of discipline. If Johnny hits his brother Jamal in the head with a baseball bat because Jamal called him a dork, and all Johnny gets is a "shame on you" scolding, that's probably not an appropriate correction, particularly if Johnny has been spoken to before about controlling his temper. Similarly, if Sarah was not paying attention and dropped her doll on the floor and you tripped over it, grounding Sarah till she's thirty is overkill.

The goal of all discipline is not to punish but to help your child become all they are capable of being. And discipline, when administered properly, communicates in a powerful way to your child that you love them. Don't wait around for them to say "Gee, thanks Mom for disciplining me." That's not going to happen. However, most people who were well disciplined as children look back with great affection and appreciation for their parents. They recognize that the discipline they received was a clear indication that they were deeply loved—even if they felt no compulsion to express that at the time it was administered. As a parent, you have the responsibility to discipline your child. Trying to provide loving discipline from the position of being your children's friend—as opposed to being their parent—almost never works. Simply put, part of loving your children is to provide correction for them.

> *Expect their respect when they are young, and enjoy a lifetime of friendship.*

The core truth to glean from this chapter is that if you parent when your children are young, you will have them as friends for life. If you strive to be their friend as they are growing up, they will likely wind up as adults who act like children. Expect their respect when they are young, and enjoy a lifetime of friendship. Seek the friendship first in the wrong season, and you may lose their respect for a lifetime.

Chapter 13

Being Friendly but Not Friends

"I FEEL LIKE EVERYONE IS ALWAYS JUDGING HOW I DISCIPLINE MY KIDS."

A COMMON SCENE IN comedies is a character who plays a non-typical or unhealthy role in another character's life. For example, the school teacher becomes the love interest of the parent of a student, or your doctor becomes your karate student. These situations make for good comedy, but such role reversals don't make a good family story. Parents must remain parents and kids must remain kids.

My son went to his high school prom recently. A friend of ours, Carolyn, stopped by our home a few days later. Carolyn had a daughter who attended the same high school and went to the prom as well. We were sitting around the kitchen table when Carolyn commented that she was glad the prom was over.

"Why?" I asked.

"Well, because the whole prom scene makes me nervous. I just don't know what sort of trouble with drinking and boys my daughter might get into."

Carolyn went on to say how she pretty much just gave in to her daughter's wishes to spend prom night at the hotel where the dance and dinner were held and didn't have any real curfews or boundaries that she required of her.

My son Jason happened to overhear our conversation and later made this comment to my wife: "She doesn't really want to know how her daughter behaved because she doesn't really care."

"Why do you say that?" I asked.

"Well because if she cared, she wouldn't have just let her daughter do whatever she wanted."

The mom "gave in" to her daughter's wishes and wanted to please her. My son did not view that as an act of love, which I'm sure was her motive, but as an act of ambivalence. My point in sharing this story is simply to illustrate that regardless of how much your son or daughter may whine about the rules you set up and the amount of discipline you provide, they innately understand that discipline (if done properly) is an indication of the love, respect, and care that you have for them.

My son Pearce is an avid outdoorsman, especially when he can combine the outdoors with risk-taking or guns. I joined his paintball team for a regional game that took place in the Ocala National Forest. Although I really don't enjoy being shot with hard, welt-producing balls of paint, it was an opportunity to spend time with him and his friends. I was fairly successful and had quite a few "kills." After the game, I was eager to hear my son's approval and mentioned my successes and strategies several times on the way home. During a lull in conversation, Pearce said, "Dad, do you remember how you told me that girls don't like needy guys? Well, kids don't like needy parents." Ouch. He just called it as he saw it. I was seeking his approval, his admiration, his friendship.

Kids need and desire to be parented. They need (and despite their protests to the contrary desire correction, structure, direction, and love from their parents. They need friendship from their peers.

Discipline is not about simply controlling behavior, but is an incredible act of love you provide to ensure that your son or daughter's character and confidence are shaped and refined to their full potential. Remember, there is a dark side of discipline where the discipline is more about releasing your own frustration than providing loving correction and training for your child. Following are some discipline principles to guide you in your quest towards shaping your great family story:

> *Discipline is an incredible act of love you provide to ensure that your son or daughter's character and confidence are shaped and refined to their full potential.*

DISCIPLINE RULE #1: CONSISTENCY COUNTS

One of the hardest aspects of parenting is being consistent. My child's room can be a mess twenty-nine days out of the month but Lord help him on the day I've "had it" and suddenly decide to enforce the rule that your room must be kept clean. Part of creating a "safe zone" in your home necessitates that children know what's expected at all times, regardless of how you feel or how busy you may be.

Remember what we established in Chapter 1: consistency counts. You need to be trustworthy with your child. Being trustworthy means that he or she will be able to predict your reactions to their behaviors.

Exceptional Inconsistencies

Perfect consistency will never be found in your house or mine, but wise parents try not to confuse their children. Even so, following are some acceptable examples of inconsistences from Dr. Marilyn Heins.

- Parents can usually tolerate some degree of disorder but want the toys cleaned up before a party. Kids can easily deal with this and even get into the party spirit with you.

- A parent can handle usual and normal household noise levels when feeling okay, but not on a day when a headache is throbbing. Children are naturally empathetic and can easily learn to quiet down because Mommy doesn't feel good.

- There will be times when parents ordinarily explain the pros and cons of an issue, but there might also be times when parents have to say, "Do what I tell you right now, I'll explain later!"

- Parents should change their minds when they get new information. You might find out that guns are unsafely stored in your child's friend's house and tell your child that house is now off-limits.

- Although safety and "no hitting" rules must be enforced by everybody, there are many people who interact with our children like grandparents, baby sitters, teachers, etc., who have different ideas and standards about other aspects of child behavior. It is not only okay but desirable for your children to figure out that Grandma does not allow kids in her living room or that the teacher insists that shoes be worn at all times. One of the most important lessons children must learn is how to deal with, and react appropriately to lots of different people.[17]

DISCIPLINE RULE #2: DON'T THREATEN WHAT YOU WON'T ENFORCE

A cardinal rule of providing effective discipline is to not threaten consequences that you are not prepared to enforce. When you threaten your daughter that she won't be allowed to go to the prom if she sasses you one more time, are you really prepared to follow through on that threat? Or will you succumb to the tears, tantrums, and the pressure of being the meanest mom in the world?

When you say you will do something and then you don't follow through, you are essentially training your kids that what you say really doesn't matter. Kids are amazingly shrewd in their ability to "work" you over. They know your weak spots, how to push your buttons and get you to back down. So don't lay

---

[17] Dr. Marilyn Heins, "Consistency," AllParenTips website, posted August 23, 2013, http://parentkidsright.com/consistency.

down a threat of consequence that, if you're honest, you know you won't enforce. Be careful not to overstate consequences. If you do make a hasty or irrational statement it is better to pull back than to stick to a consequence that is unfit for the crime.

Positive Correction

We've all seen or heard parents who scream at their child in a public place like a shopping mall or a grocery store. Sometimes children can become exasperating, and if we're not careful we can find ourselves venting our frustrations onto a child no taller than our kneecap.

Consider how the following responses may change your tone of voice and influence your child to try to please you.

Negative Responses	Positive Responses
Stop running	I'm looking for a walker
Stop screaming—You're too loud	Use your inside voices
No jumping	Jump on the grass, not on the couch
Eat all your vegetables	Take five bites—let's count
Calm down—settle yourself!	Lay your hands on your chest and say, "Peace." Good. Now do it again.
No hitting	Take his hands into yours and say, "God made these hands to do good things!"
Don't take that from her	Model sharing—use raisins at snack and do "One for you and one for me. I am sharing."
Stop arguing or I'll send you both to bed.	OK, love just went out the window. Let's sit on the couch

People not only learn from their mistakes, they learn more effectively from their successes. Most of the time children only need a little positive redirection to set them back on course.

DISCIPLINE RULE #3 WHEN POSSIBLE, GO WITH CONSEQUENCES OVER PUNISHMENT

This is the way the real world works. Our son, Skylar, developed the habit of locking his bedroom door when he would become angry or annoyed with us. The problem was that he often had trouble unlocking the door and he would fall asleep with his door locked. Our concern was that, as a child with special needs, he would become panicked in an emergency and not be able to free himself from his bedroom. We told him that he was always free to close his door, but he must stop locking it. When he continued to lock the door, we simply, without ceremony, removed the door knob. Months later, he asked to have the door knob restored; we replaced the door knob, and have not had an incident since that time.

I'm a wing-it kind of person. Wing-it people do their best work "on the fly," being spontaneous. While being spontaneous is a virtue in many circumstances, it is often not an asset when parenting. In order for your discipline to be effective you have to clearly and consistently state the rules of the house. In short, plan ahead. Post them on the refrigerator door, or if you must, wallpaper their bedroom with the house rules. Get your kids to initial and sign the rules chart if need be—do whatever you have to do to take away from your kids the excuse to defend themselves by saying, "I didn't know that was what you wanted."

But in all fairness, don't assume that just because you think it, or you said it once in a particular situation, your child knows that's the rule for all time. For example, let's say you just washed the windows and your child opens the sliding glass door by putting both hands on the glass to slide it. You correct him for smudging the glass. So is it now a rule that hands cannot be placed on the glass door or is it only a rule the day after you spent the weekend cleaning the windows? Don't assume your child knows.

The converse is also true. Let's say you have a rule that prohibits eating in the family room. But while enjoying a movie, you have the urge to eat popcorn, so the kids get to do so as well. No sweat. But does that mean that eating their Cheerios in front of the tube while watching Saturday morning cartoons is now okay?

> When you dole out a punishment for a bad behavior or attitude without forethought, you are likely to do so in anger or perhaps overstate or understate the consequence.

The point is this: don't assume anything. Communicate your rules clearly and consistently. Do it verbally—and in writing when possible. Get kids to acknowledge that they heard you. You can shout at them as they are heading out the door for school that they have to do their homework when they get home. Did they really hear you, or were they tuned out?

Make sure you get them to acknowledge they heard you by both a visual (nod) and a verbal (yes Mom, I hear you) response. Even so, they are still going to be in denial half the time. That's normal. Getting them to acknowledge you is not just for them but also for you. You need the assurance that you really did tell them so that three minutes later when they swear they never heard you, you can be confident that they did.

Just as it's important for children to know what's expected of them and what good and acceptable behavior is, it is equally important that they know in advance what will be the consequences of breaking the rule or failing to meet the acceptable behavior. Here's where the "winging-it" style of parenting can get you into trouble. When you dole out a punishment for a bad behavior or attitude without forethought, you are likely to do so in anger or perhaps overstate or understate the consequence.

You can't always settle everything in advance. But as much as possible, try to let your child know up front what would be the consequences for breaking the rule. You know the old saying: an ounce of prevention is worth a pound of cure.

DISCIPLINE RULE #4: DON'T DISCIPLINE OUT OF ANGER

Just because your child makes you crazy sometimes does not make you a bad parent. It makes you normal. Life can be a pressure cooker sometimes. Even calm, low-key, unflappable moms and dads lose their cool from time to time. But when you're frustrated, hurt, or angry is not when you should discipline.

If you need to send your child to their room or to sit in the corner while you calm down, do that. But don't lash out of your anger or hurt. You will likely spew hurtful and nonhelpful words and perhaps threaten a punishment that either is out of line with the offense or something you will ultimately back down from and not enforce.

Most of us were raised by imperfect parents, had imperfect childhoods, or less than ideal previous marriages, which means we have baggage. Kids have a way of bringing to the surface some of our own issues, fears, and insecurities. So it's understandable that when a child does something that triggers a hot-button issue with us, we tend to react badly. Just remember, your kids don't know about your past or your issues. Even if they did, it's not their problem to deal with, it's yours.

Don't parent out of your hurt but rather let your parenting be with purpose and from your strength and conviction. We all have baggage, but try to be in touch enough with your own heart that you are aware of the triggers that set you off. For the sake of the kids, work on your issues. No matter how dysfunctional you may have been raised, you have the power, the ability, the opportunity, and the obligation not to pass those same issues on to your kids. You need to be man enough, or woman enough, to break the cycle of hurt. Let it end with you. What a gift you can give to your children—what an inheritance.

They can be raised in a healthy, loving home, never having to suffer and deal with the issues that you faced earlier in life. You want the best for your kids. So don't saddle them with baggage from your past.

DISCIPLINE RULE #5: DON'T ALLOW KIDS TO TRIANGULATE

It's amazing to me how intuitive children are. I was talking to a new friend recently who came to me with some questions about parenting. His kids were pitting mom against dad, working the system.

This is not an uncommon issue as you might imagine. I asked him how old his kids are. I assumed they were teenagers. I was shocked when he told me they were one, three, and five. Imagine—even toddlers can figure out to go to mom if they don't like the answer they get from dad.

If you are a single mom or dad, you are not immune from this issue, at least if you have joint custody of the kids. It can be heartbreaking to try and enforce rules only to have your ex ignore or undo them during visitation. The only way to stop the triangulation is for mom and dad, whether living together or not, to get together away from the kids and agree together that you are not going to let the children "work" you like that.

You can agree together on who will make the call in various situations. You can agree that whenever your child asks you something your first response will be, "What did your mom say?" or, "What did daddy say?" Make sure the child knows that if they lie to you, then the answer becomes "no." Understand that there will be times when you and your spouse disagree on what's best for the child or how discipline should be handled. Work it out together in private, not in front of the children.

DISCIPLINE RULE #6: ADAPT THE CONSEQUENCES AS NEEDED

You have to experiment and find out which types of consequences work best with each child. As your child grows and matures, the methods and consequences you use should change. Some kids are motivated by money, so threatening to take away their allowance becomes a big motivator. For other children, money just is not a big deal to them.

Other possibilities could include losing privileges such as going out with friends, using their phones for social media, having a sleepover, or being able to ride the bike, or skateboard. Then of course there is time-out or doing extra chores.

Some children respond better to positive motivation for good behavior rather than negative consequences. Threatening to take away a month's worth of your daughter's allowance for failing to clean up her room may not work nearly as effectively as offering to double her allowance for the month if she goes the whole month without you once having to remind her to clean.

The goal of a parent is to raise kids who understand they have a path they were created to pursue—that their lives were created by design and with intention.

Just remember, with positive rewards you don't want to get into the habit of paying for behavior that should be expected. Use it as a tool to get your son or daughter into the habit of doing what's expected. Otherwise, if they are smart and work the system, they'll be rich and ready to retire by the time they are nineteen, and you'll be broke (and broken in spirit).

Some of my kids are pack rats, and their rooms looked like it. Even when I had them clean their rooms, all that was produced were closets stuffed with junk so that nothing was laying out on the floor. Then I came up with the idea of "poundage." I told the kids I would pay them ten cents a pound for anything they cleaned out of their room. Guess what? They came up with three to five kitchen trash bags each, full of old school papers, unused toys, and school projects from four years ago. We went to Publix, our local grocery store that had big scales out in the foyer of the store (the kind you could stand on to weigh yourself) and weighed all their trash bags full of tossed junk. I think the adventure may have cost me $10 (yeah, do the math . . . a lot of junk), but it was worth it.

DISCIPLINE RULE #7: BE RATIONAL AND INSTRUCTIONAL

The goal of a parent is to raise kids who understand they have a path they were created to pursue—that their lives were created by design and with intention, and thus they are sacred, have value, and are called to make a difference in the world. Therefore, we need to convey to them that discipline is a critical part of helping them grow into the full measure of their potential. Your house rules—and the consequences for breaking them—are part of the script of your family story. Your role is much like that of the director who is trying to get the best out of the actors on stage. The rules and discipline are there for a reason. Help your children know why the rules are what they are. "Do it because I said so," should never be the first or even second response to their questioning. There is a reason and a purpose behind the rules, and the rules are there expressly to help that child become all that he or she was designed to be. Remember, kids developmentally don't think the same as adults. Toddlers have no intellectual capacity to embrace reason. Even elementary age children have only limited cognitive ability to think in terms of reason until their early teen years. So while it's proper to want to be rational and instructional when disciplining, explain on a proper level that your child can understand.

Yes, there are some rules of the house that are purely for my convenience (such as, "don't interrupt me when I'm working in the office"). But mostly the rules are to help them, not me.

Even rules like "don't interrupt me when I'm talking to you" are not given merely for my convenience. But I know that in life, learning how to hold your tongue for an appropriate time is something they need to learn—that to be successful, they have to learn to listen before they speak.

The rules are almost always to help them achieve their potential. Don't hesitate to tell them this. Oh sure, especially as they become teenagers, your kids will let you know that they don't care about the whys, and they don't need a lecture. But trust me. They hear and retain more than you think. You'll be amazed one day at some of the things you'll hear your kids say that they appreciated about how you raised them, just probably not while you are still raising them! It's important for kids to know that you are intentional about the rules you set, that there is a reason behind them, and that reason is always for their benefit.

Obviously there are going to be necessary limits to your explanations. If you ask your five-year-old to stop asking if he can go ride his bike, because you're going to eat dinner in ten minutes, you realize that they have virtually no concept of time. So when you get the inevitable "but why?" response, you may give a brief attempt at a rational explanation, but don't keep going on for the whole ten minutes, trying to reason with the child. I'm sure it's situations like this where the infamous "because I said so" phrase was born. The point is, your five-year-old doesn't need or really want a rational explanation. Go ahead and give him one— but only one. After one explanation, training your five-year-old that obedience delayed is the same as disobedience becomes the bigger issue. Make sure they know that you are not discussing it further, and if they attempt to discuss if further with you, they won't ride their bike again for three days.

Chapter 14

The Motivation Behind Discipline

"HOW MANY TIMES DO I HAVE TO TELL THEM SOMETHING BEFORE THEY GET IT?"

LIFE IS FILLED with disappointment. Life is unfair. Your kids will have difficult teachers, in-laws, bosses, and co-workers who don't like them or who treat them unfairly or are unkind. A crucial part of your child's character development is teaching them how to respond to discipline and criticism. Philosophers talk about a wise man being one who embraces correction, but the fool who will not accept discipline (see Proverbs 12:15-16). People who can handle constructive criticism and correction most always do better in life than people who reject or refuse to be corrected. Discipline builds our character.

Disciplined people typically get things done, get recognized for their achievements, are happier and more self-confident, and often outperform their peers.

How do you learn to be disciplined except by being disciplined? Discipline is not just a punishment for bad behavior, but when administered properly and with love it becomes a high form of training and instruction. Discipline becomes a profound expression of love and to withhold discipline is to withhold love.

> *Discipline becomes a profound expression of love and to withhold discipline is to withhold love.*

Learning to handle disappointments and how to respond when we don't get our own way is an essential character-building aspect of growing up and becoming a successful adult. So your failure to provide your child with lots of opportunity to receive instruction through discipline will stunt his or her emotional and spiritual growth as surely as one's failure to exercise and eat right will limit physical potential.

It takes discipline to win at life. Athletes need discipline to compete. Students need discipline to study. People in the workforce need discipline to succeed and get ahead. The time to learn discipline and have your character shaped by sound discipline is not as an adult, but as a child. A person taught a second language as a child can pick it up so much easier than an adult trying to learn a new language. Discipline was intended to help us be all that we can be, and it is designed to be administered most effectively by a loving parent as a child grows and matures.

Family landscapes are peppered with stories of parents whose children outwardly adhered to the rules, the family values and principles while they were at home, but as soon as the kids had freedom, their behaviors changed radically. How many former Disney child stars, held up as role models to young girls for their wholesome image and appropriate dress grew up and seemingly jumped off the deep end? I specifically remember watching an interview a few years ago with a popular seventeen-year-old star and her father. She stated that her family had helped her to retain perspective on her prosperity and that she was grounded in values that she had been taught. On a recent awards show, her behavior was so provocatively outrageous I could not help but wonder how many children were hurriedly shuttled out of the room when she appeared. Once she became an adult and began making all of her own choices, her past persona became only a memory. The values we were led to believe she was raised with and embraced as a youth no longer appeared to be guiding her choices.

For several summers I helped to lead a group of teenagers on a trip to a socio-economically challenged part of Philadelphia. Every summer, one of our tasks was to help paint over the graffiti that had been painted on the outside walls of an inner-city church. I asked the pastor if it wasn't frustrating to be fighting this same battle year after year. He explained to me that although it was annoying, he understood what truly lay beneath the paint. It was not a blatant desire to desecrate or destroy his church, but the desire to make a difference that could be seen. He explained that many of these kids would never live more than five miles from where they were born. A large number would never know what it was like to make a true impact in the world, but this was their way to make a small, tangible mark. It was also a way to be a member of a group, to belong. I definitely don't endorse defacing property, but I respected this man's insight. He knew that the wrong behavior was being motivated by a true need for validation. Sometimes bad behaviors are motivated by legitimate desires, just as there are often good and acceptable behaviors that belie illegitimate motives.

Teens need to feel that they "fit" somewhere, that there is a niche in which they belong. The desire is not wrong, but kids need to be directed where they fit and where they belong. If this does not happen at home, then parents have no control over where it does happen. My point is simply that to tell a better story, when correcting your child you want to address not just the outward behavior, but the heart—the internal desires and longings that are motivating the behavior. Aristotle tells us that we are teleological beings—we do things, however inappropriate they may seem, to move us in a specific direction or to meet a specific end. As parents, it is imperative that we understand what our children's behaviors are telling us about what is motivating them. To correct only the behavior and ignore the appropriate longings can be a behavioral battle won and a heart battle lost. The child psychiatrist Dr. Rudolph Dreikurs suggested in his book *Children: the Challenge* that there are four basic reasons that children misbehave. There may be many more, but for the sake of this book, let's examine his material.

Kids misbehave to:

1. Get attention
2. To get power
3. To get revenge
4. To frustrate you enough to leave them alone.[18]

---

[18] Rudolph Dreikurs and Vicky Soltz, *Children: the Challenge*, (New York: Penguin Group, 1964).

Without some awareness of the motivation, you may be rewarding and encouraging the opposite of what you want encouraged. For example, if a child is misbehaving for attention and you only focus on their behavior, and give them your attention, you are reinforcing their misbehavior. It is my experience that this happens regularly in grocery stores. The child is screaming for a fruity, sugary cereal. Rather than pass that cereal and make a better choice, some parents will give in for the sake of others around them. The child's behavior is reinforced because he received his goal, so you can be certain that the next trip will produce the same scenario.

Remember, the goal of children is to get their own way. It is helpful to be curious about what is motivating their outward behavior. You can never know the full motivation of someone, but the screenwriter of a good story is always looking for the signs of what might be the core belief that is driving the actions of the characters.

It always amazed me when my children were young that my wife understood their cries—whether they were anger, fear, want of affection, or hunger. Quite frankly, they all sounded the same to me. She developed a keen curiosity and was successful at discerning their needs. Although it is appropriate to meet all of the desires of infants who do not know how to manipulate, that principle changes quickly as the child ages. The motivations of an older child are often much more difficult to discern.

When my son Skylar was about fifteen, my wife discovered something odd while cleaning his room. She found a stash of Brazil nuts that had been hidden in a sock and then placed in a plastic bin. Our family knows that my wife loves Brazil nuts, and she had been asking what was happening to all of them as they continually disappeared. Mona was irritated to find that he had been hoarding the nuts, especially since he did not like them. She sharply questioned him about the purpose, to which he replied, "I hid them because they are special." Since he commonly hid things that he deemed as special, we knew this was the truth. My wife could instantly understand that this inappropriate behavior had a positive motivation. At that point, we validated the motivation and taught him the proper way to express this desire to protect things that are special. We explained that he should ask the person who considers the object to be special how they wanted it treated. He understood.

It is much more difficult to spot unhealthy motivations when the behavior has an outward positive appearance. At first, teens with eating disorders simply look as if they are very disciplined with their eating and exercise, but the root motivation is not health. It is control—to deal with a broken image of themselves and beauty. A parent might inadvertently reward or continue to encourage "good behavior" when what they are actually doing is rewarding their child's self-contempt and need for control.

What about the girl who begins wearing provocative clothing? By simply making her change her clothing, you may win the battle but lose the war. While enforcing the value or behavior you deem appropriate in terms of her modesty, you are not addressing her cries for attention or giving her the validation she is seeking through the approval of boys. Does she feel invisible? Are the clothes simply stylish, or do they make her feel more desired by the opposite sex? Do you need to ensure that she understands that she is valued and cherished and that she should never compromise her own comfort level to gain the attention of others?

Much human behavior boils down to simply wanting to feel significant, special, and safe. These are all legitimate and valuable desires. The younger someone is, the more likely they will have a difficult time matching their desires with the appropriate behavior. At the same time, the desire to be noticed is not an immoral or bad desire. If there is an area of your child's life that seems to have dominance over every aspect, be it athletics, music, academics, physical beauty/fitness, gaming, martial arts, etc., it would be wise to become curious about their motivation. Is their present preoccupation a means to an end, or do they feel as if they are not strong enough, worthy enough, smart enough, or important enough to be cherished? Depending upon what you discover, you might want to direct your kids to a healthy group of kids to spend time with.

It is not uncommon for a child who isn't a superlative of some sort to lower their personal standards until they find a group in which they fit. Remember, belonging is a core value. I think it is especially important to help your kids find a group that they can fit with as they enter high school. Be it sports, band, clubs, debate, or whatever, it is important that your child not fall into that "unknown zone" where they will seek out any group, good or bad, to feel as if they belong.

A sign of maturity in an adult is the ability to connect the heart and head, and understand why you do the things you do. Kids and adolescents do not naturally connect the heart and head. So one of your tasks as a parent, especially as your adolescents develop the capacity for abstract reasoning, is to help them recognize the goals, dreams, and hopes beneath their behavior. When their behavior is unacceptable, lead your children to healthier ways to address the underlying motivations.

An effective parent is as concerned about the motivation as they
are about the behavior.

There is an exercise at the naval academy in which partici-
pants enter a special pool that simulates the inside hull of a boat.

> *An effective parent
> is as concerned
> about the motiva-
> tion as they are
> about the behavior.*

As the "boat" begins being flooded with
water, the captain has two major decisions
to make. He has to keep the ship afloat by
bailing out the water but must simultaneously seek the source of the problem. It is
a balancing act. If you have a child who is
struggling with a problem that is pulling
them down and they are in a proverbial boat that's sinking, you
want to help them not only bail water but also plug the leak.
Bailing is an effective strategy only for the short term. If all you
do is constantly bail (correct the behavior) eventually you (and
the child) will simply get tired and give up.

If we only correct the behavior without discovering the source
of the problem, eventually the child and parent will sink from
pure exhaustion. If the obese person attempts to lose weight
and deals only with the behavior of overeating, they will have a
temporary and moderate success. However, if they address the
behavior of overeating and simultaneously work to discover and
seal the hole in their boat (the causal factors that energize the
overeating), they should have more long-term success. If you try
to deal only with the core internal issues and not the behavior,
the ship will sink because it fills up too fast. A good captain
will live in the balance between bailing water and fixing the
leak. A good parent will live in that same tension. As you direct
some of your energy to changing your child's behavior (bailing),

you need to simultaneously try to understand the core desire that your child is experiencing and expressing (fix the leak).

Many adult problems can be traced back to when they felt shame and guilt for legitimate longings as children. Our daughter Rachel grew up with her biological family. She did not become a member of our family until she was seventeen years old. It has been a thrill, delight, and mystery to live with her and try to unravel some of her motivations. When we recently celebrated a family birthday, Rachel drove in from the university she is attending, bought the makings for a cake, made a card, and was ready for the big day. It was my birthday, and I simply wanted a nice, quiet family dinner. We went to my restaurant of choice, returned home, and I opened my presents. A little while later, Rachel began acting stand-offish and aloof, not at all the festive behavior we would have expected or deemed appropriate for the situation. We asked her several times if there was a problem, but she assured us that everything was fine. My wife had an epiphany. We knew that all holidays were very important to Rachel, because she was never able to celebrate them as a child. Mona simply asked Rachel, "You are hurt because you wanted this day to be a bigger deal, didn't you? You wanted it to be really special." Rachel wrapped her arms around my wife's neck and started to cry. She was not being aloof because she was angry, but because she was disappointed. I am special to her and she wanted my day to be special. Her motivation was pure and lovely, but her actions did not match her lovely heart.

Please understand me when I say, that good motivations are not an "excuse" for bad behavior. When your son or daughter acts inappropriately, you need to address that. Just don't settle for dealing only with the outward behavior. Look to the heart. Discern the inner motivation that is propelling the behavior that needs correcting and be sure to address that as well. Appropriate desires and longings should never cause your children to feel shame; they should be addressed and met appropriately. But as you discover the longings and motivations, change the inappropriate behavior.

Connecting—The Theme of Your Family Story

Chapter 15

Connecting with Traditions and Moments of Impact

"I JUST WANT TO GIVE MY KIDS BETTER MEMORIES THAN THE ONES I HAD GROWING UP."

A THEME IS THE central topic, the idea or the point that is central to your story. The theme of a family story told well is "connecting." In difficult family stories, the theme might be survival, hopelessness, despair, or loneliness. However, if you desire to shape a family story that is healthy, loving, significant, and makes a positive impact on the world, your theme should be connecting.

I once took a group of students to China. We were in Beijing when that country was experiencing its largest snowstorm in fifty years. Unable to get to our final destination and with limited resources, this could have been the most frustrating day of our trip. As we were walking across a snow laden Tiananmen Square, I sensed a growing discouragement among the students; I suggested that we drop to the ground and make snow angels. This is a place of great historical relevance and I told them that they would be some of the few people on earth who had made snow angels there. As we rolled around on the ground there was much laughter and we were inundated by locals who took pictures. Years later, if I happen to see some of those students, they don't mention the teaching that we accomplished, visiting the great wall of China, or the people they met who live secret lives; instead, they laugh and tell the story of the snow angels. I like to think that scene provided a memory for some of the nationals who stood beside us and took pictures. It was not a life-altering event. There were no earth shattering truths or perspectives shared. It was simply a moment, a moment of connection, a moment punctuated with something out of the ordinary that became memory.

The moments that shape us are those when we feel alive, when one or more of our senses is heightened. Sometimes these are moments filled with fear, anger, or disbelief. But if we are fortunate, more often they are moments of awe, joy, and inspiration. Many of the best moments don't just happen. A wise parent would do well to look for opportunities to create them. They are usually moments with high emotion, high warmth, some vulnerability, and fun.

I recently talked with a friend who said, "Never skimp on vacations." You can do without the new car or the expanded wardrobe. But set aside time and money to take your kids on a

memorable vacation. Why? Some of your child's fondest childhood memories, will be moments that connect them to their
sense of identity with the family and perhaps even to God. Are
vacations the only way to have these experiences? Of course not.
Is it common for families to not have it in their budget to take
a vacation every year, or even every few years? Certainly. But
the point is not to focus on a fancy vacation, but rather focus
on finding ways to make memories and moments of connection
with your kids. Don't feel you need to spend a fortune and take
your kids to Disney World for the moments to be memorable.
Quite the opposite—sometimes the simple traditions and magical moments (like the snow angels in Beijing) become important memories.

Moments that become memories create connection. They
often involve spontaneity and thinking out of the box. If we
happen to be in Knoxville, Tennessee and drive by the Hyatt
Regency, my son Skye always remembers the elevator races
we had in that hotel. I was simply trying to think of ways to
entertain him to give my wife a break, but he thought they
were exciting. On a bright, summer day my wife decided that
it would be fun for our young sons to paint the outside of our
sliding doors with their fingerpaints. Once the painting was
finished, she simply sprayed it off with a water hose, but it
became a memory.

We travel to Maine most summers and each of my sons
remember the days I would wake one of them up early in the
morning before anyone else was awake. We'd "sneak" out of
the cottage where we were staying and drive a short distance
up the coast to where the Pemaquid Lighthouse stands. We'd
knock on the back kitchen door to a small restaurant called the

Sea Gull Shop that overlooks the rocky coast and ask the cook to let us buy a donut and some juice even before the restaurant was open. Then, we would head out to the craggy rocks and find a perch high above the waterline and watch the swelling waves crash with majestic splendor against the vertical pitch of the rocklike. We would come close enough to the edge that we would almost catch the mist from the ensuing spray. I'd make up adventure stories as we would eat our early morning breakfast and then do some climbing along the rocky coast. It is seldom the most expensive vacations that create memories. It's the little things, the personal times, the "moments" you create that make those wonderful connections.

Of course, as our children age, the events that stick must change. We had a large group of teens come over one year on New Year's Eve. In need of some activities, we created the New Year's Eve Olympics and used toilet paper rolls to make trophies.

Some important moments cannot be contrived, but must be taken advantage of at a moment's notice. After my son spent a summer as a whitewater rafting guide, he invited me to come up to North Carolina for a weekend. Two years out of high school, he was trying to solidify his identity, his faith, and the direction in life that he wanted to pursue. One of the highlights of my life was when he led me down the river as my guide that day. I was impressed with his command of the raft and the passengers, and his knowledge of the river. His sole focus was that everyone remained safe while having a great adventure. The unseen, unspoken story that was occurring on that boat was a subtle shift in my relationship with him. At some point as a boy moves into manhood, he must take on his father and win. On that day, my son demonstrated that he knew that river and how to guide far better than I ever would. It was a rite of passage, one which we did not plan, but one that we embraced.

The importance of rites of passage can be quite significant. I've done a rite-of-passage ceremony at our family cabin in the woods of Maine with each of my sons as they turned fourteen. One small but important aspect of that signal event, is that prior to the ceremony I would typically refer to my sons as "my boy." However, after they go through their rite-of-passage ceremony, I never again refer to them as a "boy." My son is now a man, a young man mind you, but nevertheless, I am diligent to be sure I always refer to them as "my son" or as a man, never "my boy" or even as a teenager. Our family has been intentional in not referring to our children as teenagers when they entered that stage of life simply because the term, while accurate, is almost never complimentary. Think about it, when is the word "teenager" ever used in a positive light? In our home we had boys who became men.

Many cultures have a rite of passage where a young man or woman is formally initiated into adulthood. This type of ceremony can be incredibly affirming. What does it mean to be a "grown-up"? How do you know when you are no longer a child but have become a man or a woman? Parents can help their child make the transition from childhood to adulthood by having a ceremony, typically held between the ages of twelve to sixteen, when the parent formally acknowledges that their son is no longer a boy but a man or their daughter is no longer their little girl but a young woman. Go to our website, www.nextgeninstitute.com to download examples of rite of passage ceremonies and events that you can adapt and use with your child.

MOMENTS TO TRADITION

There were several times when "one-time" events became requested traditions. When our sons were young, we had a trampoline in the backyard. That trampoline became much more to our young family than just a place to jump. On summer evenings, we would lay on it and look at the stars. During warm days, we would place a broken sprinkler beneath it and keep cool while jumping in our swimsuits. Even during the cold days of winter we would slide on the ice atop the trampoline before cracking it.

I decided to take my preschool boys out one evening to give my wife the opportunity to relax. When they asked why mom wasn't going, I explained that Waffle House was a special place for men to eat their favorite foods: bacon and waffles. We decided to rename Waffle House "Man Town." I had no idea that twenty years later, I would still be taking my twenty-five-year-old son there to eat. Some traditions stick. The servers there have always been kind to Skye. People will be faithful to those places where they feel alive, and will often want to replay those events.

Some of the most memorable moments often take place in times of transition for your children. During transitional periods it is important that you seek out opportunities for conversation. As my son was transitioning into high school, I decided that we should eat breakfast together once a week. I am not suggesting that many of the conversations were full of rich, life-changing events. Many of them were simply about the high and low points of the week. I don't believe that any specific breakfast was memorable, but the consistency of eating together each week showed him that I took an interest in his life. After a few months, he knew that if a question arose about anything in his life he could share it with me at our Sunday morning breakfast. One of the simplest, yet most powerful things I did with each of my children was blessing them every morning. We read in the Bible how the great patriarchs like Abraham and Jacob laid their hands upon their children and spoke a prophetic blessing upon them that would carry on through generations. Almost like an inheritance, the child received a blessing from his father that was special and unique to that child.

For years, it never occurred to me that this patriarchal practice had a modern-day application for me as a parent. Once I got hold of the idea that I could not only teach my children spiritual things and pray for them, but I could intentionally bless them, it became a key component of my parenting philosophy.

So every morning, as I took the boys to school, before they left the car to head to class I would pause, lay my hand on each of their shoulders and one by one bless them. It was nothing elaborate mind you, just a short blessing where I would speak something over their life. These blessings were often opportunities to deposit into the mind and heart of each son some measure of the character and destiny that I believe God desired for them. Blessings spoke not just of the short term, such as, "may you have a good day, make a positive difference in someone's life, and remember the algebra you studied last night," but more often spoke about their future and called forth a vision of their future, such as, "may you discover and practice the leadership gifts that you have received."

Think of the last novel that you read. There were probably moments, turns, events, and phrases that are memorable. Here are a few tips on how to create a feeling of connectedness.

New Experiences

New and novel experiences create connection. Take your son or daughter on their first camping trip, to a Broadway play, or simply to the lake to go fishing. When you experience an event for the very first time, memories are made.

Working Together Toward a Goal

Common tasks that have been mutually agreed upon create connection. Your kids want to spend a day at an amusement park, but there is work to be accomplished first. Bring the family together and let each member participate in the plan for completing the task. If the garage must be cleaned, let everyone agree on who will sweep, sort, box up, throw away, etc., all of the items in the garage. If they plan and execute as a team, they will feel more like a team.

Make Ordinary Feel Special

Sometimes a memory is made simply because you did an ordinary thing in an uncommon way. For example, in our family, waking up Christmas morning to open Christmas presents has become something of a legendary experience because of what we refer to as the "Christmas Tunnel." This tradition started when our sons were small. One year while visiting Grandma and Grandpa's house for Christmas, my wife's parents put one of those vinyl collapsible tunnels at the bottom of the stairs for the kids to crawl through before getting to the presents under the tree. Well, not to be outdone, I thought to myself, *I can improve on this.*

So the next year, I visited the loading docks of several department stores and brought home scores of boxes which I linked together with packing tape to make a tunnel that went from our foyer, through the kitchen, around the dining room, and into the living room, finally dumping out next to the Christmas tree. Since I'm a guy, the obvious challenge each year is to outdo last year's tunnel. I should have never started this tradition. Over the years, the Christmas tunnel tradition has expanded to the point that recent editions included chutes out the second story window, multiple trap doors, and a "decoy route" that took up the entire front and side yard, in addition to multiple rooms inside the house. Two hundred boxes all assembled on Christmas Eve means I didn't get much sleep! But my kids have a family tradition unlike any other, something that's uniquely their own and I suspect will likely be continued when they have kids. (I will be available as a design consultant for my sons but look forward to getting a good night's sleep while they stay up all hours doing construction.)

Dream Together

Sharing dreams and emotions can also create connections. Does your child feel safe sharing their dreams with you? Do they know that you will help them talk through these dreams and help create a plan to reach their goals, or would they expect you to reject their aspirations as silly, meaningless, or out of reach? If they can't discuss this with you, they will find someone else.

I have a friend whose daughter, Olivia, has dreams of becoming a well-known actress. She dreams of starring in blockbuster movies and eventually receiving an Academy Award. Her father is a financial planner and is very aware of the financial ups and downs that his daughter's dreams will probably create. He loves her deeply, but cannot understand the dreams of his artistic daughter and does not truly believe that they are reachable. He is motivated by the desire to protect her from disappointment and heartache, but she experiences his suggestions of a more "reasonable" vocation as a rejection of her dreams. The result has been tension in their relationship. She now speaks to others of her goals, and does not include him in "the loop" of her activities. If he had shared his caution with her initially and then used his abilities as a planner to help her chart her way, I believe their relationship would be quite different today.

Vulnerability Creates Connection

As adults, there are times when we feel rejected, unappreciated, and unacknowledged. Our years on this earth have helped us develop strategies to cope with these situations, but you will be your child's first teacher in this arena. If he has been bullied at school, will he be too embarrassed to share with you? Has a foundation of unconditional love been laid deeply enough that they know that you will not mock them or simply tell them to "suck it up"? Have you been appropriately vulnerable with your child by sharing similar difficulties and how you dealt with them? If your child is able to share with you their shame, embarrassment, or insecurity, a deep, memorable connection can be created—a connection of trust.

Appropriate Physical Touch

We all need physical touch. I have found it interesting that even though my son with autism does not like for anyone to touch him, he will occasionally seek some physical connection. This usually lasts for only a moment. He might lean on my wife's shoulder or occasionally reach his foot over to touch her foot if they are both watching TV. Children need to be held, cuddled, kissed, tickled, and even gently wrestled. Experiencing frequent, expressive and appropriate affection in the form of physical touch will not only help your child to understand what is appropriate but will create an emotional connection with you. Hold them while you read and they will associate reading with warmth and safety. If you are married, let your children see you hug your spouse. Surrounding them with appropriate affection will begin the process of helping them to identify what is true affection and what is illegitimate.

Focused Time

We have all heard the slogan "it's quality, not quantity." While I agree that quality is extremely important, you also need quantity to establish trust. You do not need a four-hour block of time in which you intently stare at your three-year-old. If you are discussing it now, why do you say there is another time for this discussion? It could simply be twenty minutes of time when that child is your only focus. Turn off the TV, let the phone take a message, read social media at a later time. Your child will know the difference. Let your daughter hear you say, "I'm sorry, but I will get back with you later. I am spending some time with Olivia right now" and you will instantly see that little girl grow a little more confident of her place in your heart. Do you have four kids? Grab one to walk to the mailbox with you, and ask about their day. Reserve one morning each week for breakfast, and take a different child each week. Ask your son to accompany you to the grocery store, but surprise him with a run through Dairy Queen first. You will have to plan, grab, and wrestle those moments, but those singular moments can make a lifetime of difference to your child.

So find the moment. Seize the moment. Pour into your child one moment at a time. Why? Because when you turn around, they will be grown and on their own, and those moments will have formed the foundation for their relationships for the remainder of their lives.

Chapter 16

Connecting with Heritage and Heart

"I DON'T KNOW HOW MY PARENTS DID IT!"

I RECENTLY SPENT TIME on a trip to Honduras with a friend Andrew, who also happens to be a good friend of my son David. On the first leg of our trip, Andrew pulled a ragged hat out of his backpack. I made a comment about the hat and asked Andrew about it. He drew a wide smile as he held out the hat to say "this hat was my grand-dad's hat. I take it with me on every overseas trip I go on as a way to remember and honor him." I thought to myself, "How cool is that?"

Andrew's grandfather lived a life of such significance that two generations later, his hat is still a symbol of honor and inspiration. I share this story at the opening of this chapter to encourage and challenge you to take time to think beyond the moment, to recognize that some of your most significant acts may live well beyond your children to bring meaning and blessing to your children's children, and their children, and potentially to several generations beyond you.

All of us have a deep need to belong, to know that we are not just here for the moment but are part of something bigger than ourselves. Having a sense of heritage can be a very powerful part of your child's identity and self- worth. Take time to let your children know where they come from—your family history. Share tales about grandparents, great-grandparents. Talk about the struggles and conquests of previous generations that are unique to your family story. Challenge them to live a noble life, one that will enhance the tradition and heritage that future generations will inherit from them. In our live-for-the-moment, instantaneous society, this notion of heritage and tradition may seem antiquated or worse, irrelevant, but it is a critical aspect of human development that a conscientious parent will want to develop. Children need to know that they are part of a family heritage and that their story will matter to generations after them. This aspect of childhood development is often overlooked by parents. In the past, children, parents, grandparents, and great-grandparents not only lived in the same town, they often lived on the same property and sometimes in the same house. Children had the benefit of hearing firsthand about their family heritage and history. These moments and memories helped shape their character, their personality, their confidence, and identity. The

Turn off the TV, let the phone take a message, read social media at a later time. Your child will know the difference.

industrial revolution began the process of disconnecting families. And that trend has only increased as our lifestyles have become increasingly fast-paced. Many of the things we think are connecting us are actually pulling us apart.

I recently met a friend for lunch at a local restaurant. I looked a few tables over and saw a group of about five women all sitting together at a large round table. It was apparent that there were three generations at the table, at least one grandmother, perhaps a couple of daughters and what appeared to be two middle-school-aged granddaughters. You'd think, "How cool to see three generations of ladies all meeting together." I agree. The only problem was that instead of actively engaging in conversation with each other, they were all staring at their smart phones, busy texting someone other than the very people they had set aside time and space to meet.

Now that my sons are adults, I enjoy listening to them fondly remember the family traditions Amy and I gave them. These are the very same family traditions that they complained about when they were little. I recently spent some time with my brother and we laughed together as we reminisced over all the chores our dad made us do. My dad was a stickler for detail and what most would call a "neat freak." For instance, my job was not just to "cut the grass." Oh no, I was to "manicure the lawn" which meant not just cutting the grass, but edging the driveway and sidewalk and pulling weeds. If I didn't meet my dad's standard, I got called back to finish the job. I was convinced that if I didn't wash my bicycle after every usage, *including* using chrome polish on the chrome rims, that the bike would rust and fall apart. (Do you have any idea how difficult it is to have to polish around all those spokes?) Why? Because my dad was insistent that if I wanted something to last I had to take care of it, and that meant always putting my things away clean. I am happy to report (in case you were wondering), that bicycles work just fine dirty. But my brother, sister, and I shared this common heritage which gives us a sense of identity. And even though none of us inherited that extra "neat-freak" chromosome, that heritage does help define who I am as a man, a husband, and a father and I am grateful for it.

Okay, so maybe your heritage was not so great. Maybe your dad was an alcoholic. Maybe your mom abandoned you. Of course you don't want to pass on negative traditions to future generations. But perhaps you can use the negative aspects of your childhood to fuel your determination to start a new tradition. I have some dear friends who both came from really dysfunctional families. Alcoholism, abuse, a turn-style of men in and out of the house. Neither Carl nor Madison had any sense of normalcy in their childhood. Yet, this couple have been happily married for more than twenty-five years. Having a difficult upbringing need not sentence you to a dysfunctional adulthood. You can make choices to live better than how you were raised. You can begin a new story from which your future generations will derive benefit and blessing.

> *Instead of actively engaging in conversation with each other, they were all staring at their smart phones, busy texting someone other than the very people they had set aside time and space to meet.*

The point of this chapter is to encourage you to take a longer view of life. Building a positive story is not just about seeing your own children become healthy adults, but playing your part in extending or starting family traditions, a heritage that will bring meaning and blessing to future generations well beyond your own sons and daughters. Help your children connect with their past and find life, value, meaning, significance, and satisfaction by embracing all the positive aspects of their heritage—things that they will want to pass on to their own sons and daughters.

Chapter 17

Connecting with the Divine

"I'M NOT GOING TO PUT MY VALUES ON
MY CHILD. I WANT THEM TO DECIDE FOR
THEMSELVES WHAT THEY BELIEVE."

A GOOD MOVIE CAN be set in a small town with a simple cast and pedestrian premise. The movie *Life as a House* is one of my favorites. George Monroe is divorced, estranged from his kids, and diagnosed with terminal cancer. In the process of building a house, not only are his own familial relationships mended, but he also enriches the lives of others in the town. In the same way, the well-written story of a family does not simply connect the characters within that small story, but it also affects the lives of others in a greater community. In a corrupted world, selfishness separates us from others, creation, and God. A good story redeems and restores this connection.

191

Most good stories are about redemption. Corrupted humanity is separated; redeemed humanity is connected. When redemption is a part of our story, it frees the best of what we humans can be—kind, generous, and empathetic. The task of writing a better family story is to move each cast member toward redemption, which is synonymous with connection. In this final chapter we will wrestle with what most would consider the ultimate connection—connection with the Divine.

Our purpose in writing this book is to help you write a better family story. The grand story of all humanity that has been shaped and shared since the beginning of time is one that answers the questions, "Why am I here? Why do I exist? Does my life matter?" These questions ultimately lead to a quest for God. The small story of our individual lives becomes big when we see it played out as part of this wondrous, grand story of meaning and purpose. You are attempting to shape a family story. Your family story only makes sense as it plays out in the context of a scene or chapter of the larger story. Humans wrestle with their significance as part of the grand story of life in which God is the author. We are cast members in this divine narrative—the objects of His pursuit and affections.

While there are many religions in the world, our discussion for this final chapter will be written from a distinctly Christian perspective. Even if you don't agree with us on these matters, you can still find insight and value in the principles we discuss even if you don't apply them in the same way.

We live in a created universe on a planet created by a living being. This grand, divine being created a world that allows us to be in relationship with one another and with him. Just as our children are born foolishly thinking that their way is the best way, humanity turned its back on God's plan and created a world based on greed and selfishness. Much like a parent who has a wayward son or daughter who will do most anything to see that relationship restored, God has a deep longing to redeem His creation back to Himself. Since your child was made for relationship and connection, it makes sense that a crucial role of a parent is to see each member of their family restored in relationship to the God who created them. This is the ultimate redemption story. Each of us begins this divine journey in a corrupt and harsh world and moves through it with the belief and hope of a new world where all will be made new. In short, you approach life and parenting differently when you realize we are all only passing through our extremely brief time on earth in a fabulously flawed human condition. As we said earlier, most good movies and stories that capture our attention are about redemption, because your story is ultimately about redemption. When we first discovered that Skylar had special needs, my wife and I grieved. He would never play on a football team, sink the winning shot on a basketball game, follow his father's footsteps into academia, marry, have children, or produce grandchildren. Honestly, those truths can still sadden us. But my wife and I both understand that our highest goal is for each of our children to know God and walk in alignment with the story He has written.

The "Golden Hour"

In graduate school I befriended a young man who grew up in Castro's Cuba. He recounted a story from when he was in third grade. Some government officials entered his classroom. They instructed the children to "put out your left hand, close your eyes, and ask God to put a piece of candy in your left hand. Now hold out your right hand and ask Castro for a piece of candy." At this point, the official would place candy in each child's right hand. They knew that they were not just fighting for the children for that day, but they were trying to shape a generation's belief about government and God in the market-place. In the same way, advertisers of adult products (beer, cig-arettes, etc.) have long targeted children in their advertising. They know what many parents don't—that if you want to influ-ence a person's belief system, you should focus on influencing their beliefs while they are young.

Most trauma surgeons will tell you that when a person has a life-threatening accident, there is a "golden hour" immediately following the incident. If victims can receive medical attention during this brief window of time, their chance of survival is dramatically enhanced. In the same manner, recent statistics from a Barna Research Group nationwide survey pointed out that 73 percent of Americans who have a personal relation-ship with God through Jesus Christ have that initial experience before the age of eighteen. In fact, the probability of people "finding God" is only 6% once they reach adulthood.[19] Clearly the "Golden Hour" of time for shaping a person's values and beliefs is childhood.

Whose Job Is It Anyway?

Whose job is it to teach your children about "truth"—the church, the school? No, it belongs to us, the parents. You can send your kids to church camps and Christian schools, but you

---

[19] Adapted from *Raising Spiritual Champions*, Gospel Light, 2004.

should not outsource the responsibility for their spiritual development. Church pastors and leaders can help, but they are no substitute for an engaged parent.

Your kids need to grow physically. You can send them to soccer camp, give them tennis lessons, and rely on all sorts of experts and other supporting cast members to help your child develop physically. But you are the only one who can kick them off the video games and make them go outside and play. You are the only one who can ensure that they get a healthy diet of fruits and vegetables and not just consume junk food and artificially processed food. You have a profound influence on your child's physical health.

You send your kids to school to receive an education and intellectual training. But if you never read to them as a preschooler, if you don't insist that they do their homework, if you don't care whether they bring home acceptable grades, then you are shirking your responsibility to shape their intellectual growth and health.

> *You can send your kids to church camps and Christian schools, but you should not outsource the responsibility for their spiritual development.*

Likewise, don't assume that others will take care of your child's spiritual life.. You can draw upon the skills and expertise of others, but always know that the moral and spiritual training of your child belongs to you alone. Don't assume that educating them is the responsibility of your school, church, or government. The responsibility to train your child in the way God has designed her belongs to you. Your kids need to be trained spiritually, as well as physically and intellectually. They need their spiritual character formed right along with their bodies and minds—they need their spirits trained.

Guidance for an Amazing Life Journey

Life requires guidance. Builders need a plumb line to know the walls are straight. Roads require guardrails to set the boundaries for safe travel. Hikers need a compass. Young people need mentors, athletes need trainers. Most road trips whether across the town or across the country are helped by a GPS navigation system. It's not a matter of whether or not you need direction and guidance, the decision is where you turn to find it. Each of us needs a compass to live by: a set of guiding values, principles, and beliefs that guide our thoughts, decisions, and actions. The Bible was written in part to give us this compass. Giving your kids a "biblical worldview" can be an essential part of writing a good family story. It's an essential part of raising and training them. The time to help your child form his or her worldview (biblical or otherwise) is while they are still under your care.

According to the Barna Research group, what a person believes by the age of twelve is largely what he or she will believe for the rest of life.[20] Why do you think Hitler created the youth camps to train young people in his ideology? Why do you think Muslims take young boys and require them to memorize the entire Koran as part of their education? Why did Jesus say, "Let the little children come to me"?

Matthew 6:33 (NLT) says, "Seek the Kingdom of God above all else, and live righteously, and he will give you everything you need." Memorizing Scripture is fine, but does your child understand what it means to "seek the Kingdom of God" with the accompanying assurance that everything else needed,

---

[20] George Barna, *Transforming Children into Spiritual Champions* (Ventura, CA: Gospel Light, 2003).

God will supply? Are you demonstrating how to live out that priority in your own life? While it is possible for parents to say, "I'm not going to force my beliefs on my child. I'm going to let them decide for themselves what they want to believe," the reality is that parents need to be the primary examples of living in relationship with God and teachers of that relationship if children are to embrace it for themselves.

Here are simple strategies you can employ:

Pray regularly for them, and train them to develop their own ability and desire to talk to God.

Teach them God's Word, the Bible. Start when they are small toddlers by reading to them basic Bible stories such as Adam and Eve, Noah's Ark, Jonah being swallowed by a fish, Jesus lying in a manger, Jesus walking on water, angels helping Paul escape from prison—there are many stories in the Bible that will capture a young child's heart. As they grow, expect them to advance in their understanding of Scripture beyond just the cool stories.

As a family, be involved in a like-minded faith community. Prioritize worshipping together as a family. Your children will know how important the spiritual dimension of life is by seeing the importance that you place upon it. This can be in a corporate, traditional church building or in a smaller gathering in your home.

Live the Christian life in front of them. Help them to view life through the lens of Scripture. We must help our children discover the amazing plan that God has for them, and teach them what it means to follow this plan rather than live for themselves.

This is the great battle, the great decision that all of us need to make. Do we do what we want or what God wants? Living for one's self is a wide highway filled with enticement and destruction—lots of wounded and broken bodies, lots of tragedies line this road. Living for God is a narrow path. A marvelous path that He created just for them before they were conceived—the path of purpose, significance, and joy that will bring them a life of meaning and fulfillment for as long as they live.

An important part of our spiritual development is making meaningful connections with our neighbors. In 2004, Hurricane Charley ripped through Central Florida. We lost power for days. Downed trees blocked access to our neighborhood. My son Samuel and I helped our neighbors by handing out ice. We also invited them all to bring their gas grills over and we all cooked the incredible food that would otherwise spoil in our freezers and refrigerators that were quickly thawing without power. Instead of letting our food spoil in our homes, we shared dinner with our neighbors and made a wonderful connection with them. We are connected to people when we serve alongside others and serve others, working for a greater cause. Part of writing a good story is helping your children make connections with others.

Being the best parent and having a wonderful family story is still secondary to being a great person who is personally connected to God.

A word of caution—in your zeal to write a great family story, don't become guilty of making a secondary goal of primary importance. What do I mean by that? Being a great parent is important. Shaping a great family story is important. But being the best parent and having a wonderful family story is still secondary to being a great person who is personally connected to God.

The key challenge I want to leave with you as we wrap up this book is that a critical aspect of shaping a positive and enduring family story is that you are intentional in training up the whole person—body, mind, soul, and spirit. Raise your sons and daughters with sharp and agile minds that are curious and eager to learn. Teach them the importance of having a healthy body, and the conviction to do their best to keep it that way. Inspire and cultivate the character traits that will make the world a better place—traits such as courage, compassion, resilience, empathy, determination, kindness, and fearlessness. But also train them to be able to sense the presence of God, to respond to His teaching and will, and to recognize that they have been given a heavenly destiny that will give them hope when they face difficulties in life.

Epilogue

Happy endings

S O WHAT DOES it mean to write a great family story? What does the finish line look like in the challenge to raise children well? As we've seen, it's not about raising kids who get good grades, make a lot of money, marry the right person, and give you lots of happy grandbabies. All those things are nice and important, but they are not the ultimate goal.

Writing a great family story means raising sons and daughters who understand that they were created for a purpose and have a healthy relationship with God, with themselves, and with others. Writing a great family story means raising children who recognize their unique gifts and who will use those gifts to help others live better lives. Writing a great family story is about raising children who live their lives to experience significance, purpose, and joy. When a person lives this way, life may not be easy, and he or she may not be rich or famous, but a person with such a perspective can live a life of no regrets.

Your children can grow up to bless you and be a blessing to you. You will grow old being a satisfied person, knowing that you have shaped an incredible family story, one that will live and love on for generations to come!

Continue the
Conversation

If you believe in the message of this book
and would like to share in the ministry of
getting this important message out, please
consider taking part by:

- Writing about *Shaping Your
  Family Story* on your blog, Twitter,
  Instagram and Facebook page.

- Suggesting *Shaping Your Family
  Story* to friends and send them
  to the author's website www.
  nextgeninstitute.com

- When you're in a bookstore, ask them if they carry the book.
  The book is available through all major distributors, so any
  bookstore that does not have it in stock can easily order it.

- Encourage your book club to read *Shaping Your Family Story*.

- Writing a positive review on www.amazon.com

- Purchase additional copies to give away as gifts.

———◆———

To request either of the authors to speak
at your next event, contact us at:

**info@nextgeninstitute.com / 407-563-4806 /
www.nextgeninstitute.com**

Shaping Your Family Story
Small Group Study

AVAILABLE FALL 2016.

A great way to find strength and encouragement as a parent is to be part of a small group with other moms, dads, single parents, step-parents, and even grandparents who are walking the same journey with you.

The principles and ideas shared in *Shaping Your Family Story* are best embraced in the context of community. That's why we created *Shaping Your Family Story* not only as a book but as a 6-session small group study you can do with neighbors, friends, through your local church, civic group, daycare, or school.

The small group study includes:

- a copy of the book
- an interactive guidebook
- 6-video segments to watch as part of your group
- audio files to listen to while you're in the car or at the gym
- a facilitator's guide on how to start, promote and lead a small group
- promotional material you can use in announcing your group and inviting others.

For more information and to order go to our website: www.nextgeninstitute.com.

Help Encourage and Inspire Other Parents

Next Generation Institute developed *Shaping Your Family Story* to encourage and inspire overworked and overwhelmed moms and dads with sound parenting wisdom that will help them be the best parents they can be.

BUT WE NEED TO DO MORE...

Our goal is to inspire a generation to discover the purpose, power and promise of being a parent—not just a parent who gets by but one who experiences the thrill of making a positive difference in the lives of their children and in the world!

WE WANT TO:

- Expand our Website and Blog with more articles and support material we offer for FREE

- Host inspirational Parent Events in cities all around the world

- Provide insight and encouragement through the Media, specifically radio, television, digital and print media.

This vision and mission takes a team of people who believe in the incredible importance of parenting. If you are one of those people and would like to help, please consider making a generous contribution. Next Generation Institute is a non-profit, tax exempt 501(c)3 organization. Please join our family and help by making a generous donation. You can give online or contact us by going to our website at: www.nextgeninstitute.com